Ishtar Rising

Ishtar Rising

or, Why the Goddess Went to Hell and What to Expect Now That She's Returning

by
Robert Anton Wilson

FALCON PRESS
GOLDEN DAWN PUBLICATIONS
LAS VEGAS

International Standard Book Number:
Falcon Press 0-941494-83-8
Golden Dawn Publications 0-9622452-2-4
Library of Congress Catalog Card Number: 88-080927

First Edition 1989
By Falcon Press/Golden Dawn Publications

Book Design, Typography and Production by
Studio 31/Royal Type
27 West 20th Street • Room 1005
New York, NY 10011

Photo Editor: Harry Widoff

Cover Painting by Sallie Ann Glassman
Cover Design by Studio 31

FALCON PRESS/GOLDEN DAWN PUBLICATIONS
1209 South Casino Center, Suite 147
Las Vegas, Nevada 89104
1-702-385-5749

Manufactured in the United States of America

Contents

To the women of planet Earth
this study of unity in duality

"To the little boy in me, I am a God, you are a Goddess.
To the little girl in you, you are a Goddess, I am a God.
To the God in me, I am a little boy, to the Goddess in you.
To the Goddess in you, you are a little girl, to the God in me."

John Lilly, M.D.
The Center of the Cyclone

It was the sad time after the death of the fair young god of spring, Tammuz. The beautiful goddess, Ishtar, who loved Tammuz dearly, followed him to the halls of Eternity, defying the demons who guard the Gates of Time.

But at the first Gate, the guardian demon forced Ishtar to surrender her sandals, which the wise men say symbolizes giving up Will. And at the second Gate, Ishtar had to surrender her jeweled anklets, which the wise say means giving up Ego. And at the third Gate, she surrendered her robe, which is hardest of all because it is giving up Mind itself. And at the forth Gate, she surrendered her golden breastcups, which is giving up Sex Role. And at the fifth Gate, she surrendered her necklace, which is giving up the rapture of illumination. And at the sixth Gate, she surrendered her earrings, which is giving up magick. And finally, at the seventh Gate, Ishtar surrendered her thousand-petaled crown, which is giving up Godhood.

It was only thus, naked, that Ishtar could enter Eternity.

R.A.W.
Cosmic Trigger

Introduction to the 1989 Edition

I—The Underworld Journey

> *Midway through my life, I found myself in a dark woodland . . .*
>
> —Dante, *The Divine Comedy*
> (beginning the Descent to Hell)

In Ternberg, Austria, in 1987 I met Diane Wolkstein—we were both speaking at a Folklore convention—and she gave me a copy of her new translation of the ancient Sumerian epic of Inanna, a work dated at around 2000 B.C.E. (*Inanna, Queen of Heaven and Earth*, Rider and Company, London 1984). I was entranced by the beauty of the legend and by Diane's skillful translation, but I was also amused to find that the Inanna story was earlier than the sage of Ishtar yet basically identical to it. You see, I had known the Ishtar epic since my high school days, and, indeed, my first long poem was based on it, but I am so ignorant of Near Eastern archaeology that I had never learned that Ishtar is a late re-telling of the tale of Inanna.

The story of the moon-goddess who descends to Hell and rises again, whether she be called Inanna or Ishtar (or Persephone, or Brigit), has later, Patriarchal echoes in the myths of Osiris, Attis, Dionysus, Christ, and many other sun-gods (including Joyce's *Tim Finnegan*.) It is also, of course, the structure of Dante's *Divina Comedia*. This archetypal death/resurrection, in either its female or male forms, is called the Underground Journey by Jungians, and I recently observed, with the same sort of shock you get when you first see yourself on TV, that every single one of my novels is based on some variation on this primordial legend.

All of my heroines and heroes go through a withdrawal from tribal "consensus reality"—a journey through the realm of fantasy, horror and the Unconscious—leading to a rebirth or resurrection; many of them literally have to pass through a dark tunnel (Babcock in *Mask of the Illuminati*) or a cave (Sigismundo in *The Earth Will Shake*) or sail an underground sea (the whole crew in *Illuminatus*)—although this symbolism was not conscious when I wrote the books. ("Chinatown" plays the role of the Underground Kingdom in *Schroedinger's Cat* and "Chapel Perilous" serves the same function in *Cosmic Trigger*. The escape from the Bastille into the Upside Down Room is a surrealist equivalent in *The Widow's Son*).

Obviously, this symbolism is deeply meaningful to me, since it appeared in my first (and only) attempt at poetic epic and in all my novels. It occurs over and over in my dream diary, also; for instance, on 23 April 1968, I dreamed that I was in a Chicago nightclub patronized by gangsters of threatening aspect. Attempting to escape, I found myself on a New York subway train speeding through a tunnel; then, abruptly, I was above ground again but attacked by a mob of Ku Kluxers (although white myself, I had been involved in the Civil Right movement and has acquired some fear of white racists), but I escaped them by chanting the name of God in Hebrew, whereupon I was able to fly above their heads.

In this dream, the Underground journey is combined with the Dream of Flying (Dante meets Deadalus). Gangsters— i.e. "underworld characters"—make a nice Joycean/Jungian pun on the underworld demons of traditional lore, and the subway (called "the Underground" in England) carries associations of Ishtar's descent and of rebirth. (Tunnel = vagina, as any Freudian would say at once).

I invented none of the symbols in this dream; you will find their equivalents in the Ishtar legend, and earlier. For instance, in Wolkenstein's translation of *Inanna*, I read:

> When Inanna arrived at the outer gates of the underworld
> she knocked loudly . . .
> Neri, the chief gatekeeper of the *kur*, asked:
> "Who are you?" She answered:

"I am Inanna, Queen of Heaven,
On my way to the East."

The gatekeeper, of course, replies that nobody ever re-
turns from that gate, and Inanna continues anyway . . . like
Ishtar, and Persephone . . . and Christ and Dante and Tim
Finnegan . . .

What is striking about the Inanna epic, 4000 years old,
is that some of the words sill survive in the rites of Freemasonry. The candidate, in Dallas or Bombay or Berlin today,
comes to a door and knocks. He is asked who he is. He gives
his name and days (as instructed in advance) that he is "going
to the East." He is warned that he will never return from this
quest, and he then passes inward to the Ordeal that is the
real Initiation. Although Inanna is a goddess and female,
and the Entered Apprentice in the Craft is a human and
male, the ritual or the Archetype remains the same *after 40
centuries.* Is it not strange that, in my 1968 dream, when
threatened by Underworld "demons" I *went to the East* (moving in dream-space from Chicago to New York)? Is it not
even stranger that I knew nothing of Masonic ritual then?
Is it not stranger and more wonderful still that many Rationalist historians claim Freemasonry is no more than two centuries old?

I think all artists are prone to Underground Journeys
and Dreams of Flying—voyages far, far away from the reality-
tunnel of ordinary domesticated humanity. While I don't
totally accept the Pop Freudianism that says all artists are a
bit schizophrenic, I admit that we are a decidedly oddball
lot, especially by the standards of such official custodians of
Rationality as the Joint Chiefs of Staff or the Committee for
Scientific Investigation of Claims of the Paranormal
(CSICOP).

Pound said the artist "is the antenna of the race." Allen
Ginsberg, in one poem, called himself "the Defense Early
Warning Radar System." We myth-makers and story-tellers,
whether we be called shamans or poets or charlatans or

warlocks, have acquired the "talent" (or curse) of seeing "below the surface" and across space-time; we are all children of Hermes.

As the great contemporary Jungian, Jean Shinoda Boland, points out in her *Gods in Everyman*, Hermes is the only Greek divinity who travels between all three "worlds" of the Greek cosmos: Zeus, god of Power, remains in the clouds; Hades, god of Emotion, remains in the Underworld; Apollo, god of Reason, travels about the Earth inspiring craftsmen and scientist—but only Hermes can ascend to the starry heavens, walk the Earth, and penetrate the Underworld with equal ease. The Hermetic male, Dr. Boland says, cannot confront a border without finding a way to cross it.

(Jungians will love the synchronicity connected with this. I read Boland—and saw myself as Hermetic Male— shortly after appearing in a TV film called *Borders*, in which I articulated the view that all borders should be abolished.)

Understanding myself as a son of Hermes, after reading Dr. Boland, I came to comprehend why I dream of flying as often as of the Underground Journey and why I travel so much on the face of the Earth in my daily career as lecturer/ teacher. As a Hermeticist, I need the heavenly vistas of Zeus, which is why I study abstract mathematical sciences; but I must also re-visit the caves of Hadean (unconscious) memory periodically, because my art comes from that subterranean source; and I must travel among men and women of many cultures, like Apollo, because otherwise I might get trapped in the static reality-tunnel of the culture in which I happened to be born.

So, then: Ishtar's walk through Hell captivated me as an adolescent because it was the female image of one aspect of my own Hermetic nature; but Ishtar and Inanna are archetypes of *historical*, as well as of personal, psychological processes. The last 3000 years of history have followed the classic Ishtar/Inanna pattern: the Goddess has descended to Hell—gradually at first, as Patriarchy emerged in the early city-states, and then with catastrophic speed after Christianity arose to damn the female half of humanity of sub-human status—and now, in this century, the Goddess is beginning to arise again, through a thousand cultural transformations of which Feminism is only the tip of the iceberg.

When I read Robert Graves *The White Goddess* around 1948—i.e. about when it was first published—I recognized at once that this was to be one of the pivotal books of my life. I was sixteen then, and in no position to pass rational or informed judgments on huge historical ideas, but I had an immediate intuition, a gut-feeling, that Graves was saying something important. Scholars—Feminist and anti-Feminist— are still debating the validity of Graves' theories about early human society (and in this book I offer, tentatively, my own adumbration of a groping toward an attempt at a theory about those murky ages) but I have always felt that, whether Graves was right or wrong on specific details, he was a true visionary. He said the Goddess was alive again, and I felt in my blood that She was indeed alive: my songs were given to me by Her.

II—The Labyrinth of Deadalus

> *All men are born liars.*
> —Liam O'Flaherty, *Autobiography*
> (first sentence)

Cary Grant was once told, "Every time I see you on the screen, I think, 'I wish I was Cary Grant.' " He replied, "That's just what *I* think!"

I've been repeating that story ever since I first heard it, and it never fails to amuse audiences, all of whom seem to understand it immediately. Everybody groks that Archie Leach, the poor boy from Liverpool who became "Cary Grant" never fully believed in "Cary Grant," since Cary was, after all, his own invention. On the other hand, here's a similar story, which I also like to tell, that produces very mixed reactions, with some people laughing and others looking puzzled or slightly offended:

An art dealer once went to Pablo Picasso and said, "I have a bunch of 'Picasso' canvasses that I was thinking of buying. Would you look them over and tell me which are real and which are forgeries?" Picasso obligingly began sorting the paintings into two piles. Then, as the Great Man added one particular picture to the fake pile, the dealer cried, "Wait a minute, Pablo. That's no forgery. I was visiting you the weekend you painted it." Picasso replied imperturbably, "No matter. I can fake a Picasso as well as any thief in Europe."

Personally, I find this story not only amusing but profoundly disturbing. It has caused me to think, every time I finish a piece of writing, "Is this a real Robert Anton Wilson, or did I just fake a Robert Anton Wilson?" Sometimes, especially with a long novel, I find it impossible to convince myself that I know the answer. After all, as Nietzsche said, "there are no facts, only interpretations."

I first encountered the Picasso Parable in a little-known, virtually forgotten film, which I and a few other film buffs— damned few—consider the greatest movie Orson Wells ever directed. The film was called *F For Fake*, and, like most of Welles's work, it died at the box office; unlike most of his other films, it has not been rediscovered by the *cognoscenti* and is not even a "cult classic" yet. This seems sad to me because *F For Fake* is certainly the most Wellesian movie Wells ever made, and it was also so far ahead of its time that we only now beginning to become contemporary with it.

Fake (as I shall call it for short and to avoid monotony) is a documentary about the impossibility of making a documentary. That is to say, it does not belong in the world of Aristotle, The Master of Those Who Know, but in that of David Hume, The Master of Those Who Don't Know. It deals with magic (both kinds) and fakery (many kinds) and might almost be considered a lengthly commentary on the famous aphorism of the great Soviet director, Eisenstein— "The camera is a liar."

You will get some of the flavor when I tell you *Fake* begins with Orson doing magic tricks while asking the difference between magic and acting, and ends with a scene in which Orson, fat and old as he then was, plays a beautiful young woman and a beautiful young actress plays an old man; a scene which makes perfect sense artistically and is moving dramatically despite the violent Brechtian alienation-effect of reversing the sexes and ages of the two players.

Concretely, *Fake* is about a man called El Mir, and of course that is not his real name, anymore than Cary Grant was the real name of Cary Grant. When Wells made *Fake* in 1975, "El Mir" was living in semi-respectable retirement in Ibiza, after having served a moderately short prison term for faking Van Goghs, Cezannes, Modiglianis and various other modern masterpieces. Also living in Ibiza was Clifford Irving, who had written a biography of El Mir, proclaiming him "the greatest art forger of all time." El Mir himself brags, in the film, that most of his forgeries have not been discovered even yet and still hang in museums all over Europe and the U.S.

Of course, Irving's biography of El Mir is not entirely trustworthy; Mr. Irving, you may remember, was the man who once got a million dollar advance from a publisher for a biography of Howard Hughes, based on a contract allegedly signed by Hughes, but the Hughes' signature itself turned out to be a forgery. And we cannot easily trust the boasts of El Mir, either, since he won't even tell us his real name. The first of the Strange Loops in *Fake*, then, is that it is a documentary about a faker who wrote a biography of a faker. Welles, however, assures us at the beginning that *Fake* itself will contain no lies or deceptions, since he and his staff (he claims) set out to find, and tell, the whole truth.

By the end of the film, it is obvious that Wells was

deceiving the audience when he said that; but, of course, he has *artistic* justification for this hanky-panky. What better *form* could there be for a film about a fake biographer of a fake painter than to make the film itself a bit of a fake?

Actually, the lies that Welles reveals at the end of *Fake* are only part of the fakery he had imposed on the audience. *Fake* looks and "feels" like an Orson Welles movie, but large parts of it were not shot by him at all: he bought them from the BBC documentary department and re-edited them to give them the "Orson Welles flavor." But does this "really" make the film a fake? The cubists began pasteing newspapers and other extraneous matters onto their paintings 60 years ago; Pound inserts real letters and historical documents into his *Cantos*; Duchamp submitted a toilet bowl (upside down) to an art exhibit; Picasso once made a sculpture of a bull's head, and a mighty sinister one, out of the handlebars and seat of a bicycle, with a few bits on his own work glued on. . . .

When does a fake become "real"? Most people who have seen *Fake* believe they have *seen* Orson interviewing El Mir and Clifford Irving: actually, they have not. Welles simply edited the film so that he appears to be in the same scenes with the other fakers, and they appear to be answering his questions. In fact, they were answering other people's questions—people from BBC—and their answers are often not in reply to the questions by Welles that we hear but to other, different questions that we do not hear. Is this more "fakery" or a development of the creative editing by which, in *Citizen Kane*, people in one scene seem to be answering remarks by people in another scene, separated by years in time?

The dramatic turning point in *Fake* occurs when El Mir reflects that it is no crime to paint in another man's style; the crime only begins when the other man's signature is added. "I never did the signatures myself," he says blandly. Should we trust this convicted felon? Clifford Irving comes on screen and says bluntly that El Mir is lying, and forges signatures as skillfully as he forges art styles. "And," Orson asks quietly, "who forged the Howard Hughes signature on that famous contract?" Irving looks down—thoughtfully, or guiltily? No audience, and no member of an audience, is the final authority on what a man's face "really" reveals. (Witness any *Columbo* show.) But Irving did not look down (thought-fully or guiltily) in response to Welles' question, since Welles inserted himself and the question into BBC footage in which Irving was responding to something else. . . .

We seem to be back with the primordial Welles, the man who scared the hell out of America, in 1938, by presenting a radio adaptation of *The War of the Worlds* in the form of a series of news bulletins interrupting and gradually replacing a music show. But Welles said at the time that the news form had attracted him because much alleged news is a fictitious as much alleged drama and he wanted to explore the inter-face between *genres*.

Actually, I think, *F For Fake* recapitulates Welles' whole career and has its earliest roots in the unproduced play about John Brown which he wrote as an adolescent. In that play, Brown never appeared on stage: instead, various people recounted their own memories of the man and argued about the morality of what he did. In *Citizen Kane*, too, Kane never "appears" in a real sense, although we see Orson Welles playing Kane at various ages: the direction and format con-tinually remind us we are not seeing "the real Kane" as *ding an sich* but only a series of pseudo-Kanes recalled by people who either loved or hated him. Like Brecht and Joyce, Welles was always a non-Aristotelian artist, a post-Einsteinian.

In fact, Welles even managed to impose this Wellesian (Brechtian? Joycean?) format on a biography of himself com-pleted shortly before his death. He told the biographer that she could not write "the truth about Orson Welles" and should not even attempt that—"Do you think you're God?" he asked—and persuaded her to write the book as the story of *her attempts to discover "the truth" about Orson Welles*.

(Similarly, Niels Bohr revolutionized physics—even more than Einstein had—by asserting that the scientist can never describe "reality" but only "what we can say about reality based on our current instrument readings.")

Those readers who are not thinking of the constantly shifting perspectives in *Ulysses* at this point are probably thinking of my own novels. Like Joyce, Brecht and Welles, I have always considered the Victorian novel, with its omniscient (personal or impersonal) narrator and its one block-like "objective" "reality," to be totally obsolete and incapable of conveying 20th Century experience. All the novel (or film) of today should attempt to do is recount how various people create their own individualized reality-tunnels in their quest for that ever-receding Holy Grail, "the real truth," which exists, if at all, outside our space-time continuum.

I think it was Malraux who defined art as "lies like truth." Marianne Moore, more precisely, said poetry creates "imaginary gardens with real toads in them." in *A Portrait of the Artist*, Joyce becomes Stephen Dedalus who vows to "forge in the smithy of my soul the uncreated conscience of my race," but in *Finnegans Wake*, Joyce becomes Shem the Penman, forger (metallurgical) of alchemical transmutations and forger (illegal) of bad checks. Aristotle said art imitates nature, and what is the difference between an imitation and a counterfiet?

Andy Warhol, as is well known, used to keep a pantry full of Campbell soup cans, and if he liked you, he would autograph one and give it to you, so you could own "a genuine Warhol original." Such is the magic of art and the art of magic. The logical next step, as Hugh Kenner once pointed out, would have been for Warhol to sue the Campbell Soup Company for selling cheap imitation Warhols.

I have pondered long and hard, for many years, on the difference between "real" money and counterfeit money, and the best analysis I can offer is that we are supposed to believe the wizards at the Federal Reserve Bank have a magic wand

which turns paper into something of value, but the counter-
feiters do not own the magic wand. This can hardly be called
fakery or imposture (despite the grumblings of some right-
wing money cranks) since the Fed's notes are indeed accepted as something valuable on international money mar-
kets.

But why would a dollar become worth several million
dollars if it were hung on a museum wall by Warhol as an
example of "found art?" And would it make any difference if
such "found art" were blessed by the wizards at the Federal
Reserve or just printed in a basement by the Mafia?

Maybe humans are creatures who creates realities out
of the flux of experience by faking (imposing?) meanings and
forms? Or is that too Buddhistic a view for most of you
reading this?

Does this represent a digression from the theme of this
book, or a secret key to the book's hidden meanings? Well,
before you answer that, consider a final parable, which
comes from Aleister Crowley's *Magick in Theory and Practice*
and is said by him to contain the whole secret of practical
occultism:

Two passengers are sharing a railway carriage. One
notices that the other has a box with holes in it, of the sort
used to transport animals, and asks what animal his companion is carrying. "A mongoose," says the other. The first
passenger naturally asks why this eccentric chap want to
transport a mongoose around England.

"It's because of my brother," says the second man. "You
see, he drinks perhaps more than is good for him, and
sometimes he sees snakes. The mongoose is the kill the
snakes."

"But those are bleeding *imaginary* snakes," says the first
man.

"That's as may be," says the other placidly. "But this is
an imaginary mongoose."

And the next time you see a Van Gogh in a museum,

stop and ask if it's an El Mir. As for me, I'm already wondering if this is a genuine Robert Anton Wilson Introduction (which the publisher requested) or just another fake I dashed off because I wasn't inspired enough to write the real thing.

III—The Alchemy of Desire

Woman who seek to be equal with men lack ambition.
—Timothy Leary

I forgot to tell you that Hermes, besides being the god of border-crossings, is also the parton of puzzle-makers—and liars.

This book, like all my novels (and a few of my "nonfiction" works) was composed in the Hermetic style. This style—identified with such figures as Dante, Pico della Mirandola, Nicholas of Cusa, Giordano Bruno, John Donne, Thomas Vaughn, William Blake, Herman Melville and (in our own time) Crowley and Joyce—is the style of *F For Fake* and of Andy Warhol autographing a Campbell Soup can. The surrealist bluntly and blatantly puts a zebra in the living room, but the Hermeticist finds so many astounding things in the living room that the reader begins, spontaneously, to wonder if a zebra will turn up eventually.

The essence of the Hermetic style is to *show* what Blake claimed to see, "infinity in a grain of sand." Modern science has become increasingly, if unintentionally, Hermetic as each advance in instrumentation has shown us that there are so damned many things (and invisible fields . . .) in a living room that we better check to see if a zebra has somehow gotten in lately.

Lewis Carroll, like the surrealist, contradicts common sense. The Hermeticist accepts common sense, but carries it several steps further than we expect, subtly dragging us along on an inexorable journey to that Ineffability which is so complex and chaotic that nobody will ever imagine they can reduce it to common sense again—that ineffability which we call either Non-Sense or Uncommon Sense, depending on our personal willingness, or unwillingness, to cross borders and travel between the "worlds" of reason, emotion and intuition.

This book, frankly, got written originally because an editor at Playboy Press asked me if I could write a whole book on the female breast. "Sure," I said at once. I would have said the same if he had asked me if I could write a book on the bull-elephant's toenails. I was broke that month and would have tried to write anything, if somebody would pay me for it. When I got the contract and the first half of the advance money, I sat down and asked myself what the hell I would put in the damned book. I decided to write a treatise on the relationship of the breast to the rise and fall of Goddess religions, and—to keep myself amused, and thereby speed the writing so I could get the second half of the advance quickly—combine this with a basic introduction to Taoist philosophy, so disguised that nobody but the people who write commentaries of *Finnegans Wake* would ever figure out how many hidden meanings there were in every paragraph.

It was a lot of fun. I completed the job in three weeks. To my surprise the finished work, published as *The Book of the Breast*, sold better than either of the other two books I had done for Playboy press, received good reviews (in the places where it was reviewed at all) and seems to have been enjoyed by a lot of readers, who wrote me some nice fan letters. Nobody at all ever wrote to tell me that they had decoded my more obscure jokes or deciphered the mystical doctrines hidden between the jokes.

That suits me fine. As Aleister Crowley once wrote, "It is to be observed that the philosopher having first committed the syllogistic error *quaternis terminorum*, in attempting to reduce the terms to three, staggers into *non distributia medii*.

It is possible that considerations with Sir William Hamilton's qualification (or quantification) of the predicate may be taken as intervening, but to do so would render the humor of the chapter too subtle for the average reader in Oshkosk for whom this book is evidently written." (*The Book of Lies (falsely so called)*, Chapter 57.) I trust that this clue is broad enough to set the true Seeker on the proper path to felicity.

This book contains some churlish grumbling against the Women's Liberation movement as it was in 1972 (when the book was being written.) I have revised some passages a bit, but allowed others to remain as historical curiosities. The early 70s were the days when all the survivors of the sixties went a bit nuts, and the Women Lib nuttiness, in retrospect, was no weirder than the other screwball ideas of the time. I just mention, in passing, as an example of what was being circulated in those days, that I often amused myself by copying Radical Lesbian rants, changing the word "male" to "Jew," and then re-circulated them, asking people to guess the source of the passage. Without exception, my victims all guessed that the source was *Mein Kampf*.

Feminism has advanced quite a bit in intellectual clarity in the past 17 years and only a few relics like Andrea Dworkin still espouse that kind of attitude; but the charm of this book would be spoiled, I think, if I updated it too much, so I have retained much of my snide humor about the sexism of the alleged anti-sexists.

In conclusion, those who want to read a bit more about the relationship of the Return of the Goddess to the neurological revolution of our time—the biochemical basis of my Hermetic remarks on the crown and heart "chakras"—should certainly consult Dr. Christopher Hyatt's *Secrets of Western Tantra* (Falcon Books, 1989.)

"Abba! It is finished!"

Robert Anton Wilson

Introduction to the 1973 Edition

The histroy of civilization is the history of a long warfare between the dangerous and powerful forces of the id, and the various systems of taboos and inhibitions which man has erected to control them . . . .
—G. Rattray Taylor

The words of magic, O my brothers: Tits. Boobs. Teats. Bazooms. Thingumbobs. Knockers. Headlights. Grapefruits. Cantaloupes. A pair that stick out like Mussolini's balcony. A pair that would make a bishop kick a hole in a stained glass window. Breasts that you could hang your hat on. Yea, verily, two globes that haunt us "like the twin moons of Mars" (William Lindsay Gresham). "The latest tit lottery" (journalists' slang for a beauty contest). Even the immmortal bard himself, seeking to break out of conventional poetic language, does so by attacking the best known of all cliches: snow-white breasts. "If snow be white," he comments skeptically, "why then her breasts are dun." Joyce ends his monumental psychological novel *Ulysses* with Molly Bloom's rapturous memories:

> And then he asked me would I yes to say yes my mountain flower and first I put my arms around him yes and drew him down to me so he could feel my breasts all perfume yes and his heart was going like mad yes and yes I said yes I will Yes.

There is no art, no poetry, no song, no human expression, in which the female breast is not celebrated and adored. Its forms appear disguised but undeniable in architecture, in pottery, in the design of cathedrals and temples, in mystic symbols like the Chinese *yin* and *yang* and the European Rosy Cross. If there is beauty, meaning and consolation in the universe—as all art and worship seem to hint constantly— a large part of it is found in these strangely haunting curves. Some of the best mathematicians have been especially preoccupied with the form which is called a *double catenary* and which may have unconsciously inspired the engineers who first solved the problems of suspension bridges.

Ezra Pound, the most elusive, intellectual and politically engaged of modern poets, finally gets back to basics near the end of his 900-page, 40-year-in-writing epic, *120 Cantos*:

> How to govern is from Kuan Tze
>   but the cup of white gold in Petera
> Helen's breasts gave that

Pound refers to the old legend that a certain gold cup in possession of the royal family of Petera owed its perfection of shape to the fact that it was molded directly from one of the breasts of Helen of Troy. How to govern may be important, Pound is telling us, but appreciating such beauty as Helen's breasts is even more important. Only a man who was a poet as well as a political pundit could possibly have made such a statement—which may suggest that we would all be safer if there were more poets and fewer political pundits.

Most men, after all, are on their best behavior when under the spell of that double catenary curve; they stare or feed or caress and are as cozy as puppies—one cannot imagine them a threat to the earth, the animals or other men. But once they leave this central sacrament of existence and begin thinking about how the universe (or other people) might be improved, they are apt to go a bit wild and start brandishing clubs or cannons or hydrogen bombs. Nobody knows why the rest of us put them in government mansions instead of mental hospitals when they get stirred up that way, but they would certainly be better off contemplating Helen's breasts (or Sophia's or Marge's or Jayne's or Molly's). Earth would not resemble hell quite so much if men attended to such earthly matters more and were not up in the air over ideologies.

Aldous Huxley once wrote a book urging, among other

things, that there was great benefit to be obtained from intelligent use of the psychedelic "magic mushroom" of Mexico (*Psilocybe mexicana*). One Marxist critic commented sourly that the novelist's message seemed to be, have fun with fungi. Huxley replied sharply that having fun with fungi was better than having idiocy with ideology. I would suggest that it is better still to have fits over tits, be crackers over knockers, be bonkers over boobs, or just act unrepressed with a lovely breast.

Surely—as the pictures in this book will eventually tell you, if you look at them long enough—this must be a mad world governed by psychopaths and infested by neurotics, for many, many people will tell you that these lovely reproductions are "obscene" or "sexist" or even "sinful". Such people are a vanishing species, like the duckbilled platypus, but like all fossils they have crept into pulpits and governmental broom closets to die. They would have you believe that it would be more elevating for your character were you to peruse a book of news photographs showing the atrocities idealists have recently committed in their efforts to correct the universe.

No. Do not be deceived by such voices, whether they proceed from people actually invading your space-time right now or whether they are old tapes still playing in the back of your brain, repeating the imbecilities you heard in childhood. Beware of these false prophets—their hearts are the hearts of bats, though their faces be the faces of men. Nietzsche had the right word for them: troglodytes, cave-dwellers.

The sane and sound man, the man of *mens sana in corpore sano*, is not deceived by such leather-winged, beetle-eyed, bug-brained, cobweb-nosed, cold-hearted and muddy-intellected saprophytes, whether they march under the reactionary banner of old-time religion or the revolutionary flags of Marxian neo-feminism. They are carriers of what psychiatrist Wilhelm Reich called "the emotional plague," the spirit that denies light, the spirit that stifles life. They dwell in the shadows and in dark, clammy places, and ther is no health in them.

The most cultivated of the Medicis, Lorenzo the Magnificent (1449–1492)—banker, patron of the arts, poet, scholar—has written in his *Triumph of Bacchus and Ariadne*, the sanest of all Renaissance testaments:

> Lasses and ye youthful lovers,
> Long live Wine and long live Love!
> Let each make music, dance and sing,
> Let every heart enflame with pleasure!
> Not with duty, not with grief!
> All who live, rejoice ye greatly
> And be happy, ye who may!
> What's to come is still unknown!
> How fair is youth that flies so fast!

An anonymous Greek, 1200 years earlier, put the same message in slightly different and even more memorable words on his very tombstone to instruct the future in bold wisdom:

> Nothing to clutch in life
> Nothing to fear in death

There is no way of arguing against this ancient Mediterranean sanity, any more than you can argue with an April breeze. Those who feel it are immediately bucked up, and all your words of gloom and sin will not bring them down again. As the Egyptian Pharaoh Khati said, 2000 years earlier than even the anonymous Greek tombstone, "A man's heaven is his own good spirits."

So "be happy ye who may." Don't let them tell you that what you feel looking at these lovely pictures is "male chauvinism" or "sin" or "prurient interest," God help us; like an April wind, like the sunrise itself, like a puppy running through the shrubs, like the tenacious grass pushing up into sunlight from the most unpromising ground and even through cracks in concrete, there is one signature in all things. The force that made men out of apes is the force that makes a man stare at a nipple and makes the nipple harden proudly under his gaze.

Whitman sang of "the body electric" and hippies talk endlessly of the "vibes" in one situation and another. Freud insisted that beneath the conscious ego we are driven and navigated by a raw, erotic life-force which he called the libido. The secret Rosicrucian and Illuminati brotherhoods of the Renaissance explained all life as the manifestation of an astral energy which could be found in the sexual union by those who kept their consciousness unclouded. Mesmer, in the 18th century, rediscovered it and called it animal magnetism. Baron Reichenbach found it again in the 19th century and called it od. Whilhelm Reich, in the 1930's, showed that it could be measured on an oscilloscope attached to a man and woman in the genital embrace and now the Russian parapsychologists have photographed it and demonstrated that it accumulates in pyramid-shaped structures. Freud was more profound than he realized, when he said that the pyramids were an unconscious tribute to the female breasts.

This force—called *Tao* and *prana* and *kundalini* in the Orient, *mana* by the Polynesians, *orenda* by the Iroquois, *wakan* by the Plains Indians—is hailed as Light and Life and Joy by the poets of all languages. *It is the only rebuttal anywhere to the logic of despair.* On the level of verbal argument the cynics always win, have always won, and especially since Hiroshima must always win. The only answer to them that carries conviction is the spontaneous and unpremeditated surge of life when, always unexpectedly, Beauty and Joy manifest themselves and you know why you are here and what you must do. This illumination is always intimate, always sensual and almost invariably sexual, either in the specific sense or in a more general way. No other power can withstand the paranoiac pragmatism that constantly reminds us that we must die, that all we build must crumble, that there is no point in anything. The erotic life-energy that takes two catenary curves and turns them into the supremely beautiful and desirable is the answer, and the whole answer, to such gloomy grousing. It tells us why we go on and will go on.

Those two hemispheres are, after all, the best things in the world.

1. It began with erection

*I would have driven right by, if she hadn't had such a
beautiful pair of boobs.*
—Harold Lord Randomfactor

This hang-up that we've all got, this obsession about the
breasts, this fetish, this fanaticism, this strange compulsion,
this *worship* and *adoration*, then (let us be frank, for God's
sake—the hour is late and nuclear doom pounds on the
door: Why try to hide any longer?)—it's evolutionary, Ti-
Grace, the force of nature itself, Steinem, pure biology,
Robin. A mammal, for heaven's sake, is an animal species
in which the female gives birth to living young—instead of
just laying eggs like the birds in the air or the fish in the sea
or the reptiles in Pogo's mucky old swamp—*and then suckles
them.* I didn't do it. Hugh Hefner and Howard Hughes and
even Moses didn't do it:

Some call it evolution
And others call it God

—and that's who did it. Sixty million years ago, a hundred
million years ago, it started—a marvelously intricate biochemical process in which the governor (evolution, god,
goddess, the DNA spiral) began to transmute and mutate
blood into milk and drive it, as Dylan said, with "the force
that through the green shoot drives the flower" out of furry
little creatures (insignificant compared to the tyrannosaurus,
that walking nightmare, or the hundred-ton brontosaurus,
or their kin) into the mouths of their offspring. That was it:
It was a *milk factory*, flattish and unformed at first, just as it

still is in every species except one. Yes, we are mammals. Our ancestors were mammals. None of us arrived here in the latest mod styles or with the correct ideology and the glossiest up-to-the-minute sense of decorum and fad. No, no, not at all, baby: We emerged naked from a mammal's womb and were quickly clapped to a mammal's teat or else given a bottle spiked with somebody's notion of the correct chemicals based on something that was still the milk of another mammal—a distant cousin who says "moo" and chews grass. This is our home planet, dig; we grew here and our relatives are all over the place mooing and barking and braying and chattering in the trees. We did not drop from some plasticized, computerized, hygienic, kubrickized, anti-septic, progressive nursery in the Andromeda Galaxy. We are of the earth, earthy.

The governor intended us to be suckled; and suckled, by god, through most of our history we have been. Is this unimportant in considering our basic psychology? Grok: If you watch people carefully, you will notice a peculiar and significant fact—they are frequently engaged in sucking ac-tivities or very close substitutes. (Wait: We will see later why Eleanor of Aquitaine rode bare-breasted through the streets Jesus once walked. Hold on.) Despite the cancer terror waged by the surgeon general's office, for instance, there are still around 45,000,000 of us in America sucking on cigarettes every day. Others chew gum (spearmint, juicy fruit, candy-coated or sugar-free, take your pick), bite their fingernails, gnaw their knuckles, scrunch pencil stubs, eat a hell of a lot more than they need. (Potato chips, anyone? a Mars bar, maybe? pretzels, peanuts, cashews, do you want the cheese and crackers with your beer, mac? and do try some more of the canapes, Mrs. Miller.) Some chew their lips, gobble tranks or uppers, munch their own mustaches, yea, verily, even kiss the plaster feet of holy images—and when they get to the bedroom! Yes, brethren: Man begins as a depend-ent animal who needs to be fed for a minimum of seven months (often longer) before being able to feed himself. During these months a whole personality and a view of the world is being formed; that world-view is quite hard to change later because it is nonverbal, prelogical and probably contains large elements of *imprinting*.

Imprinting is a neural program stronger than conditioning. Normally, conditioning can be removed by counterconditioning—a dog who learns to salivate at a bell can be retrained to bark at the bell and salivate at a horn instead. Homosexuals—who are, ethologically considered, men who have been conditioned to become sexually aroused by other men; nothing more remarkable or sinister than that—have been counterconditioned, in a few notable cases, and suddenly get turned on by women, just like you and me. Such is conditioning, and if you study the emotional rush people feel at the sight of their nation's flag, and remember how they were trained to have that reaction, you pretty well understand conditioning.

Imprinting, on the other hand, cannot be removed by any amount of counterconditioning. It occurs only in the first stages of infancy, and once a reflex has been imprinted it stays for life. There is an analogy here with thermoplastic and thermosetting chemical compounds. Thermoplastic compounds can all be reversed and modified, like ordinary conditioning. Thermosetting compounds keep their shape under all conditions until they are chemically destroyed, just as imprinting remains unchanged until the organism coagulates—i.e., dies. It's nobody's fault that some natural processes are irreversible. That's just the way the world is.[1]

How important is such imprinting? Well, Konrad Lorenz, one of the most important researchers in this field, has quoted some astonishing cases. Adult ganders, for instance, do not become sexually attracted to geese unless they have been imprinted with the "program" of goose-as-object-of-affection by nestling with their mothers as newborn goslings. Lacking this maternal programming, the ganders may remain lifelong bachelors or even become homosexual. More: Lorenz tells of a case where, due to his own obsessive and protective care of these experimental birds, one gosling got imprinted with *his* image as the adorable maternal object. In adult life, this very perplexed gander followed Dr. Lorenz about like a true lover in an old balled, constantly making sexual advances, totally uninterested in the plump and more appropriate geese all around him. Stranger still, due to a series of accidents, one gander got imprinted with a *ping-pong ball* as the love object and spent his life in frustrating attempts to mount these little plastic spheres.

This may not be the whole explanation of human "fetishists," those rare types who get their jollies from women's clothing rather than from women, or from feet or hair or leather garments, etc. It is an interesting parallel, however, and it shows that "overestimation of the sexual object" (Freud's nicely cynical description of sexual love, or romanticism) is built on a firm foundation in biology. When ganders are programmed properly by their mothers, they fall in love just like humans and form pair-bonds (the prehuman origin of what we call marriages) that usually last for life. It must be admitted that they go into the woods for a little adultery now and then; Lorenz tells us of a research associate, thrilled by the discovery of "monogamy" in these birds, who was subsequently disillusioned to learn of their "infidelities." Another member of the staff then excused them philosophically with the observation: "After all, they're only human."

So: If you want to understand people, begin with that seven months of helpless dependency in which all food (and much emotional gratification, security, love, etc.) comes in only through that pair of nippled globes called the mammaries, or a close substitute. Imagine the conditioning that is obviously occurring, and the irreversible imprinting that is probably also occurring. Now do you know why you bought this book? For the same biological reason the Romans envisioned the great Mother Goddess Diana of Ephesus with literally dozens of enormous breasts (enough for everybody?) and St. Paul reports hearing people at church chanting rapturously: "Great is Diana." Great indeed! The same sort of fantasy, somewhat deflected by Christian woman-hate, appears in contemporary folk expressions about the delights of "running barefoot across an acre of tits" or, more cozily, "diving head-first into a barrel of tits."

It can be safely said that human psychology would be entirely different—radically different—if tits had never appeared in evolution. We will give repeated examples of this as we proceed. For the time being, just consider the warmest kinds of love you have experienced with other humans, sexually or platonically, with women or with men who have been friends or helpers to you. Do you think we would have any of that sort of emotion without the conditioning received at the breast? Take a look at how iguanas or other reptiles (who are not suckled) relate to each other, and make a guess about how many of the "cold, snaky bastards" you've met were either bottle-fed or nursed by mothers who had negative feelings about nursing. Wilhelm Reich said that traumas received during nursing from mothers who are uptight about their mammalian functions are "the source of the human no"—the dawn of the feeling that there's something wrong with the universe and it has to be fixed as bloodily and quickly as possible.

We don't know what sort of nursing experiences little Adolf Schicklgruber had, but by the time he was going to school Hitler already had a strong dislike of girls and grew angry whenever they tried to kiss him. Ninety million people died in the course of his attempt to correct the universe.

Womens liberationists often seem to think that the breast is rather atavistic and should go the way of the tonsils and the vermiform appendix to the dustbin of evolution. Whether they are right or not—and the author of this book can be expected to consider them wrong—the vast changes many of these ladies expect in human society probably cannot be accomplished without some such demammalization. As long as little boys (*and* little girls) are nursed at the breast, certain conditioned expectations about womanhood will be re-created every generation. These expectations, of course, do not need to coexist with systematic economic exploitation of women and can easily accommodate much more equality than is now practiced, but they sharply conflict with any attempt to create the sexless, anthill socialism the extreme liberationists want.

Actually, there is reason to believe that the distinctly human breast is a response to adult sexuality rather than to the needs of the newborn. That is, the large size of the human female breast is not an evolutionary answer to de-mands made by infants as infants but rather to the needs of these infants after they were imprinted and grew up to incorporate the breast quest into their adult sexuality. This is the opinion of zoologist Desmond Morris in his bestseller, *The Naked Ape*.

The characteristic breasts of the human female, Morris believes, are a result of standing erect. The other apes occa-sionally shamble about in a semierect position but usually go on all fours—even the gorilla leans forward and trails his fingers on the ground when upright and goes back to quad-rupedal motion when he's really in a hurry. Human beings, Morris points out, are also the only mammal species to copulate in a face-to-face position. This, it seems plausible to suggest, is because of our habit of standing to face each other during *verbal* intercourse—it seems "natural," or at least desirable, to also face each other while lying down for sexual intercourse. But the buttocks, which play a large role in sexual excitation with other apes, do not get much attention this way; *ergo*, says Morris, the human female has developed *imitation buttocks* on her chest.

Like most new ideas in science, this sounds absurd at first sight—as if we were being told that the long nose has developed as an imitation penis. Well, evolution has many such crude gimmicks (nature is a primitive artist), and it so happens that we have a biological cousin whose nose does appear to be a penis surrogate. This is the famous "purple-assed" baboon, or mandrill—the despised, evil-tempered species which plays a distinctly negative role in African folklore. (This ugly beast was even compared to the Chicago Police Department by Terry Southern during the Democratic Convention of 1968.) While ordinary zoo visitors remember chiefly the mandrill's spectacular rump, and Africans who have to live with his presence talk much about his sullen bad temper, ethologists have long wondered why his nose and cheeks are marked so as to resemble his penis and testicles. It has finally been decided that this is probably a *sexual signaling device*, on a much cruder and more direct level than the peacock's famous tail, the male deer's antlers or the beards or mustaches you and I wear to notify women, "Hey, look, I'm male!" The mandrill, true to his clumsy nature, has just found the most blatant way of conveying that message. If others "wear their hearts on their sleeves," he wears his genitals on his face.

It is undeniable that the human female breast carries the reverse message—"Hey, look, I'm female!" Is Morris correct in thinking that it was shaped by evolution for the specific purpose of carrying that signal? As Morris points out: "Other species of primates provide an abundant milk supply for their offspring and yet they fail to develop clearly defined hemispherical breast swellings. The female of our species is unique among primates in this respect." If you look closely the next time you're in the ape house at the zoo, you will see that female primates do not have, and do not need, pendulous human-style *tits*. The *tit*—note the overtones and emotional ambience of the word—is sexual, an outgrowth of the primordial teat, which was just nourishing. Morris even points out that the young, both of our species and of other apes, find it easier to nurse at small, flattish breasts. The *big* bazoom is not primarily for babies. It is for men.

Is it also, as Morris urges, a substitute buttock? This seems scientifically plausible. A man standing erect (and perhaps otherwise erect), moving toward a woman who wishes to be mounted, is confronted by the rounded curves of her breasts in much the same way that the other, quadrupedal, apes shambling toward a female of their species who is waiting to be mounted see the similar rounded curves of the derriere. Nevertheless, likely as all this sounds, it is only scientific truth, laboratory truth, and one can't keep a straight face while trying to contemplate it outside the laboratory. It is definitely not advisable to think about it in the bedroom; you might burst out laughing at the wrong time.

Imitation butt or not, the breasts certainly signal an unambiguously sexual message. When Howard Hughes produced *The Outlaw* and introduced Jane Russell to the horny American public of the 1940's, he originally advertised it by having a skywriting airplane inscribe in the heavens above Los Angeles the following tasteful sales pitch:

THE OUTLAW

Nobody had any trouble deciphering the symbolism. The demand for the movie was so great that even though censorship problems postponed its American release for nearly a decade, and we all had ample chance to inspect Miss Russell's attributes in several other films during the interlude, *The Outlaw* was still a box-office smash when the censors finally let it out with only a few cuts. Although Miss Russell later became something of a singer and dancer and even an actress by the standards of those days, and further distinguished herself by joining a very primitive Fundamentalist church and issuing such theological pronouncements as "God is a living doll," she is still chiefly remembered for the fact that from the side she somewhat resembled a filing cabinet with the top drawer pulled all the way out. Walter Winchell, the popular columnist of the period, was calling tits "janerussells"

in her honor for over a decade.

This is hardly unique. Ever since people became erect, and even though there are still many happily atavistic "ass men" among us, the front elevation of the female form (as an architect would call it) dominates sexual art and fantasy, and in that elevation the breasts are quite a bit more visible than the vulva.

More: We are in the strange position of being the sexiest animal on this planet, a fact long noted by Christian theologians who attribute it to Original Sin. In fact, as ethologists have commented, it seems to be the result of our peculiar weakness at birth and that all-important nursing period which we have already stressed so much. The newborn human cannot survive without a mother. But the human mother could not cope with the hazards and creatures of the wild, especially burdened with an infant, unless she persuaded a male to hang around and help her. *Ergo*, some form of the family was inevitable. It doesn't have to be the monogamous Judeo-Christian family, of course; it may be polygynous, polyandrous, polygamous or the "group marriage" of sexual communism in the tribe or the hippie commune, but it will be a family: A place where the young are tended until they can tend themselves.

There are many forces that can and have held families together, but the one that actually performs the lion's share of the job throughout human evolution is sex. It is that simple. Although other animals are less inhibited about sex—less mental, less worried and less squeamish—it is a fallacy to think that they are therefore sexier than we are. Anyone who uses expressions like "barnyard morals" or "acting like an animal" (to castigate a human being who seems to be enjoying sex more than the speaker) is talking nonsense. A man with "barnyard morals" or who "acted like an animal" would be much *less* sexy than the average human.

The human being is the only animal without a limited mating season: The only one who is ready, willing and able

to have sex all year long. This fact, together with our nakedness or conspicuous lack of body fur—which may also be
sexual, according to Desmond Morris—distinguishes us from
all other mammals and our closest relatives in the primate
family.

Somehow, somewhere in evolution, the proto-human
female mutated and leaped out of the estrus cycle of other
apes. She was, so to speak, in heat all year long. And this
persuaded the human male to remain with her all year long
instead of just visiting at mating time, and formed the
foundation of human society—the primordial family.

This constant sexiness or randiness may be the Original
Sin, as Fundamentalists think, but we would not be human
without it. We probably shed our fur to make our naked
bodies more conspicuous; we developed a year-long rutting
season; we huddled together into families (monogamous or
otherwise) and we became something entirely new in nature.
Without this great leap forward into sempiternal horniness
we would have remained like the other beasts.

And the sexual signaling system on the female front
elevation became the center of our thoughts and feelings.

It could hardly be otherwise. Going around on all fours,
using the normal mammalian position for copulation ("doggie
fashion," it is called by city dwellers), our ape cousins do not
get breasts involved in their sexuality. Our direct ancestors,
as soon as they stood up, began to notice the territory
between the head and the vagina, and—since love and sex
were easily merged before Christianity arose to drive a wedge
between them—this brought back cozy memories of infancy.
Women were scarcely passive about this, of course, since the
breast is a center of very strong sexual feelings, as indicated
in the celebrated limerick:

> There was a young girl from Dumfries
> Who said to her beau,"If you please,
> It would give me great bliss
> If while playing with this

You would pay some attention to these!"

On this foundation grew the entire structure of oral sexuality, to the great delight of millions through out history and the perpetual scandal of the clergy. We cannot re-create the mental processes of the Dawn Woman who first decided to give her mate a blow job, but it may well have been inspired by his own oral gratification of her nipples; some oral-genital sex, of course, appears in all animals anyway. Whoever she was and whatever her thought, she did more for human happiness than all the politicians and revolutionaries of history.

Oral sex, indeed, would be an extremely unlikely invention without the suckling experience of infancy among ourselves, our primate ancestors, and the mammals from whom we sprung. The art has been carefully (almost remorselessly) analyzed by Gershon Legman in his curious *Oragenitalism: An Encyclopedia of Techniques*, which catalogs hundreds of variations (and demonstrates mathematically that there are millions of other possibilities which the author hasn't bothered to tabulate)—and yet all of these are within the three main divisions of cunnilingus, fellatio and the 69 or *soixante-neuf*. Legman doesn't bother with the variations of breast oralism, the "trip around the world," in which the whole body is licked and sucked, or the peculiar Oriental delights of toe-nibbling and finger-sucking. A real attempt to catalog all the sexual uses of the human mouth would undoubtedly run into several volumes; if it were exhaustive in its descriptions, it could easily be heftier than a complete set of the *Encyclopaedia Britannica*.

(For instance, although sexological writers in English generally use the one word *fellatio* for all varieties of cock-sucking, the Romans had two words for two great divisions, irrespective of position. Thus, in *fellatio* proper, the man is entirely passive and the woman actively and vigorously sucks, licks and manually stimulates his penis; while in *irrumation*, the woman remains passive and the man forcibly thrusts his penis in and out of her mouth in the manner of vaginal intercourse. We are on the way to building an encyclopedia when we start subdividing these into vertical fellatio, horizontal fellatio, sitting fellatio, etc.)

Despite the deep-seated Christian aversion to oral sex (only relaxed a bit in recent decades), Kinsey found the practice widespread even during the sexual Dark Ages in which he was writing. It is hard to see how a mammal with the typical mammalian breast-suckling experience could afterward be so conditioned that oral sex would be abolished, no matter how vehemently the clergy might try. After all, as we have already seen, breast-feeding occurs when the new organism is most subject to *imprinting*, which no amount of later conditioning can alter. Nevertheless, the practice was under such heavy taboo in America before World War I that our soldiers in France were absolutely astonished at the Gallic enthusiasm for such delights—which is the inspiration for one of the best-known stanzas in *Mademoiselle from Armentieres*:

> The French, they are a funny race,
> They fight with their feet and fuck with their face
> Hinky-dinky-parlez-vous!

("They fight with their feet" refers to the popular French sport in which two males try to knock each other out using feet instead of fists. Experts at this art have been known to defeat professional boxers; they can kick as high, and as fast, as any Nijinsky, and quite a bit harder.)

Today, of course we are witnessing the amazing Linda Lovelace cult. Ms. Lovelace, who starred in a porno flic called *Deep Throat*, in which she portrayed a young lady whose clitoris was in her throat and who, therefore, could only reach orgasm through vigorous fellatio, has become a sort of heroine or fantasy figure to large segments of the population. One chap even wrote a letter to the *San Francisco Ball* saying that he had seen *Deep Throat* 17 times and was hopelessly in love with Linda. *Esquire* placed her smiling and winsome face on the cover of their June 1973 issue, but, typically, inside they joked nervously about the origin of her fame and couldn't bring themselves to say bluntly that she had performed the most esthetically exquisite cocksucking ever shown in an American movie. There is even a group in California, called the Erisian Liberation Front (ELF), which is ran Linda for president in 1976. Although they claim to be dead serious about this, their slogan sounds like a satirical comment on recent chief executives: "Let's Have a *Good-Looking* Cocksucker in the White House!"

Ms. Lovelace has even written (with the aid of a writer named Douglas Warran) an autobiography called *Inside Linda Lovelace*, in which she gives detailed instructions on how to perform *Deep Throat* fellatio ("I call it cocksucking," she says with fetching frankness). The best posture for beginners, Linda avers, is with the head hanging over the side of the bed upside-down, giving the penis a straight line to the snug warmth of the inner throat. Yoga exercises (muscle-stretching and meditation), she adds, eventually give enough control and relaxation to allow any woman to perform the *Deep Throat* fellatio in any position without gagging—although it is unlikely that any will become proficient enough to challenge Linda's calm brag: "I have become one the supreme cocksuckers of all time."

Linda's autobiography also describes a versatile assortment of techniques for getting the most out of normal coitus, anality, lesbianism and masturbation, all of which she claims expertise at. Among other benefits ascribed to yoga is Linda's claim that she can take a whole *human foot* in her vagina; and an existing porno film short shows her doing just this. (Masters of Tantric yoga in India and Tibet are alleged to perform even more remarkable feats, including continuing coitus for seven hours at a stretch and sucking the semen back in the penis after ejaculation.)

Whatever else this remarkable young woman has proven,

her career at least demonstrates that there exists a certain
force opposing the claims of the more rabid women's liberationists with their papistlike proclamations that sex is always
oppressive and degrading to women. Linda very clearly
represented the diametrically opposed viewpoint (occasionally enunciated by Ms. Virginia Johnson of Masters and
Johnson) that truly free woman can enjoy sex not only as
much as a male but quite a bit more than a male. However,
in recent years Ms. Lovelace has disavowed her past activi-
ties and professes values consistent with the anti-sex puritanical spirit of the 1980's. Perhaps she *will* become President
after all, in the tradition of Reagan and Bush.

Of course, orality has an evolutionary background. Prac-
tically all mammals practice some form of cunnilingus; that
is, the male licks the females's genitalia to prepare her for
intercourse. It never seems to go further than that, however—
at least no human scientist has reported seeing it go further.
It appears that mammals are incapable of the leap of thought
(or of energy) that allows that act to be *continued to orgasm*
and then be *followed* by intercourse. And a female mammal
fellating a male mammal to orgasm is entirely unknown.
This may actually require the evolution of a human-style
brain and nervous system, and evolution may not yet be
finished. There are already reports in medical literature about
rare and lucky women who can achieve orgasm while *only*
their breasts are being sucked, and there have even been
cases of women who can achieve climax while fellating their
men. All this began with the development of erect posture,
the transcending of the limited mating season, the use of the
breasts for sexual signaling, and the foundation of the family.

It is hard to realize that in a sense the universe has only
gradually been revealed to its inhabitants. There were long
stretches of time in which no being with eyes had appeared,
and yet everything alive was sensing and exploring its environment to the limits of its abilities. The recent research of
Backster and Vogel shows that plants and shrubs do much

of their exploring by means which, in humans, are called ESP or telepathy. (Backster calls it primary perception.) These eyeless beings also sense their world through changes in light (which can be felt) and by a gravitational sense and temperature sense, among others. Out of this evolutionary background appeared eyes and the visual space created by those eyes. So marvelous was the new universe which the eyes beheld that we find it very difficult to think of the structure of reality without thinking of it as visual. From Maxwell and Einstein to the present, modern science has baffled ordinary minds—as well as those of some scientists— who cannot imagine or deal with a reality that is not visual. Yet, on a cosmic scale, there are likely to be countless races which perceive the realities described in Maxwell's or Einstein's equations and who would regard us as deluded primitives for thinking visual reality is the "real" reality. Perhaps such cosmic minds have already evolved here, sporadically and occasionally, and this is what the great *mental* mystics like Buddha are trying to tell us.

Similarly, sex has obviously evolved from the simple seasonal program of the lower mammals to the year-round festivity that it is among humans. Among humans there are signs of slower and faster evolution also. (An old story tells of an Irishman who bedded with a young French girl in Paris. Asked how it was by another Irishman, he replied, "Sure, back in County Westmeath sex is still in its infancy!") Kinsey, in the 1940's, found that the average American male completed copulation in less that two minutes; sexual gourmets who prolong the act upward to an hour were astonished to read that. The women who achieve orgasm through breast manipulation or while fellating a man suggest powerfully that the evolution of sex, as part of the evolution of mind perception, is also continuing. So does the report of Baba Ram Dass (formerly Dr. Richard Alpert) that he has continued sexual activity for several hours while on LSD. Perhaps this is what the great *sexual* mystics like Blake are trying to tell us.

It may even be that sexual mysticism of the Blake variety—also represented in Tantric Hinduism, Taoism, many primitive religions, and by such historical figures as Jacques de Molay, Bruno of Nola, D.H. Lawrence, Walt Whitman, and Aleister Crowley—represents the growing edge of human awareness, the antennae of the species. Desmond Morris tells of a woman who could reach orgasm by having her *earlobes* sucked. Hieronymous Bosch in his paintings and Norman O. Brown in those remarkable books, *Life Against Death* and *Love's Body*, have suggested a possible evolution of sex out of the genitals into every part of the body, just as it has already evolved from being limited to one part of the year to permeating the entire year. This seems to be the direction of evolution; and Christians of the year one million A.D.—if there are any—will find humanity much more "fallen" and "sinful" than at present. From a tiny sporadic acorn, sex seems to be a tree of life growing to fill all space-time utterly.

In this evolution, the breasts are already a first outpost of the sexual energy escaping form the genitalia. They not only provoke sexual excitement in the male, they also receive sexual pleasure for the female when they are handled or mouthed properly. (Similar outposts exist in the neck, earlobes, behind the knee, etc.) The breasts represent the sexualization of a previously neutral area, and it is possible that they have been worshiped for this.

And worshiped they have been, O my brothers. The caves of our ancestors are frequently found decorated with sketches very similar to Howard Hughes's skywriting advertisement for the *Outlaw*; it is now fashionable, among some romantic theorists, to suggest that these are flying saucers. The most famous of Stone Age artifacts, the Venus of Willendorf, unambiguously portrays a woman with enormous mammaries. Similar big-breasted goddesses have been found in caves throughout Europe and the Near East. When history begins to emerge from the shadows, the earliest deities are mother goddesses, who may be considered a psychological extension of the infant's memory of the breast: They are all-giving, all nourishing and totally bereft of the stern anti-life ethics of the later father gods. Many of these deities, like Diana of Ephesus mentioned earlier, were portrayed with multitudinous breasts—an iconographic revelation of their function.

When the great patriarchal religions of gloom and damnation swept over the world, hell was invented to frighten the wits out of little children and sex became diabolical instead of divine. Men began to see the powers of nature not as gods and goddesses but as demons, and to suspect their women of being witches; and the breast was put under seven and seventy curses and exorcisms. Nevertheless, it crept back into the design and architecture of the cathedrals—as every artist knows—and eventually a new mother goddess was created and allowed to enter the Christian pantheon as the Virgin Mary.

It is important to remember that biologically we have scarcely changed at all in the past geological epoch. We still prefer to eat in our own den, and lacking this we seek a cavelike shape—which is why the wall booths in restaurants are always filled before the central tables and why the lighting is usually dim. The man of the house, as he leaves in the morning, says he is going "to bring home the bacon," although he's probably headed for an office and not a boar hunt. When we make love, we proceed from the human level back toward the primate tactile level, and the sound effects thereafter are not dissimilar to those of the great apes when mating. When we go into the woods, we travel in bands; and it has been observed that even in large sprawling metropolises like New York or Tokyo the average person has around 50 to 100 friends or at least acquaintances—the same number traditionally found in the tribal unit. Even our vaunted intelligence, about which we brag so much, merely shows our predatory history, for no nonpredatory animal has ever developed much in the way of cunning or quick wits, while our fellow predators can give us a good challenge when on their own turf and can even outsmart us on occasion. And we remain stubbornly territorial, just like our cousins the baboons and gorillas, which anybody can confirm by counting the "No Trepassing" signs or safety locks in any human community.

It has been said that one can't understand sociology fully without always keeping in mind that man originally made his living by hunting in packs. Similarly, one cannot understand sexology without remembering the humorous and serious side effects of the fact that he is an animal whose female had transferred important sexual centers from the low back view to the front top. From these facts flowed human intellect, our culture, our strange ways of organizing jobs and weddings, and above all our warped sense of humor.

There are many versions of prehistory, but I prefer to think it all began with erection. A female stood up to reach somewhat higher on the tree for a special fruit. The male looked at her and possibilities occurred to him. We haven't stopped *thinking* (about sex, and everything else) since then.

Of course, many people resent all reference to our animal genealogy. They want to believe that all their ancestors were perfect ladies and gentlemen. It is disturbing to these folks to recall that in fact most of our ancestors didn't wear ties or panties—or, worse yet, that the overwhelming majority of them weren't even mammals and looked like alligators or Gila monsters. Yet this is the record, and you can still see the frog in people when they swim a certain way or the lizard in them when they are lolling in the sun.

There is also a notion afoot in certain quarters that we have, although harnessed to this slummy and unaristocratic background, now evolved to the point where it is, or should be irrelevant to us. One might as well tell the robin that a person of his sartorial splendor should be above such grossness as eating worms for dinner. The robin, glorious as he is, is still a bird (and, if he has any sense, proud of it), and man, for all his gaudy and flashy brilliance, is still a mammal (and, if he has any sense, proud of it). Do you imagine it would be more dignified to be an ostrich or a louse or a crab? Would it be less disgraceful to have feathers like an angel (or a duck) than to have the characteristic fur of mammal? Would it be more ethereal to synthesize energy directly from the sunlight, like a dandelion, than to gnaw on bones like our second cousins the dogs? For that matter, does anybody hold it against his pet dog that the creature was born alive from a bloody womb, suckled at a teat, and scratches his coat like any other mammal? Then why, in heaven's name, feel uncomfortable when the same facts are mentioned about yourself?

It sometimes seems that we haven't yet come to grips with Freud, much less with Darwin. If somebody quotes Freud's opinion that the pyramids (which are religious temples as well as tombs) represent idealization or sublimation of the desire for the breast, somebody else will invariably snicker and remark that it just shows that the religious impulse is only a deflection of sexuality. But what does the "only" mean? Is it not an implication that religion should be manufactured of some finer energy than that which drives infants and men to grasp for breasts? Should it? What higher energy is there? We say that "God is love," thinking we have transcended the animal and material worlds with that resonant proclamation. But is there one who has not first learned of love while holding a breast between the hands or in the mouth?

We can laugh at the many-breasted Diana of Ephesus as a crude conception of divinity, and yet perhaps the Romans were *more* sophisticated than us, not less. Christian theologians may proclaim from now till the last galoot's ashore that their paintings of divinity as an old man sitting on a cloud are not meant to be taken literally (was Diana taken literally by Ovid?), but they continue to speak of "He,"

thereby giving their god a biological gender and therefore
(since we do not speak of plants or algae as he or she) a
vertebrate nature. Can we imagine this gaseous vertebrate
(Thomas Henry Huxley's phrase, and still an apt one) as
truly nonhuman and nonmammal? Try it, and see if a rather
fishy or reptilian image doesn't fill up the blank as you push
mammalian images aside. "God is a symbol of God," said the
subtle modern theologian Paul Tillich. It does seem that God
the Father, like Diana the Mother, is just an image of something else—something we cannot name but which we encounter in the family relationship and the sexual drive out
of which that relationship grows. (All gods come in families,
even the allegedly monotheistic Judeo-Christian God. Caba-
listic Jews gave him a wife, Shekinah; and Christians, even
more in keeping with Freud, gave him a virgin who is both
his wife and his mother.) This "Divine something, this DNA
spiral or governor or Tao, made Sophia Loren out of ances-
tresses who a short time ago looked like the Venus of
Willendorf and a while further back looked and walked
much like Cheetah the Chimpanzee. What it can still make
out of us staggered the imagination of Nietzsche and inspired Kubrick to produce *2001.*

Biology is much more mystical than theology, O my
brother: For, dig, out of the simple animal tit, scarcely more
than a nipple, our friend the governor (or governess) sculpted
these round, cup-shaped, gloriously esthetic human breasts,
each consisting of 15 to 25 separate lobes which are almost
whole biological systems in themselves. Each lobe contains
clusters of lobules designed as intricately and functioning as
smoothly as the best modern machinery, all protected and
made delightfully soft to the touch by large amounts of
insulation in the form of adipose (fatty) tissue. From each
lobe there flows in a great network like some master biocomputer the lactiferous ducts, running to meet in the nipple;
and without crowding or any traffic congestion, two more
networks, of blood and lymph vessels, are also packed into

these cups, providing nourishment, and thermostatically regulating temperature. Best of all, the entire system has a neat feedback loop—"the hot line," English biologist Alex Comfort nicely calls it—running down to the genitals. This hot line is activated when a man sucks or caresses the breasts, creating sensation in the clitoris which make life worth living to the lady in question and may even begin the process of vaginal lubrication preparatory to intercourse.

The same feedback loop, even more marvelously, goes into action when an infant nurses at the breast, and the pleasant vaginal sensations (which occasionally result in orgasm for some nursing mothers) also begin the process of healing the internal sex organs after the stretching and labor of childbirth. And all this operates on servomechanism principles, without the executive officer (ego) having to pay any attention at all. She can remain up on the bridge (i.e., in the frontal brain lobes) concentrating on other matters, at least until some of these processes become so pleasurable that she must turn cartwheels or bail out entirely, swimming in the ocean of bioenergetic bliss until the ship stops tossing about and she is able to resume command again. Most marvelous of all, as R. Buckminster Fuller points out in *Nine Chains to the Moon*, this servomechanism, and all the others in the female body and those in the male body too, and those in all our cousins throughout the mammal kingdom, and our second and third cousins in the fish and bird kingdoms, is not really a dead machine (as this terminology makes it seem) but a living presence, which Fuller he dubs the "Phantom Captain." This is not just an elaborate way of saying that living *organisms* are *living* organisms; it rather sharply reminds us that the executive officer we usually recognize, the ego, scarcely deserves to take so much credit when things go right—or so much blame when things go wrong.

Why do we think of the phantom captain, then, as a father or mother? Anthropologist Weston La Barre answers:

An understanding of [religion] embraces also the explanation of why religious response is uniquely human. *The context is the universally human nuclear family, the condition is individual human neoteny* [prolonged infancy] . . . . At the basis of every religion is the familial experience and all religions consequently contain some basic Oedipal story in their myths[2].

This neoteny, of course, brings us to the area of Freud and psychoanalysis, the subject of our next chapter. Before plunging into the heated and almost fetid hothouse of controversy surrounding Freud and his work, it is well to remind ourselves that whatever is true of modern infants was also true 20,000 or 50,000 or even 500,000 years ago. If modern infants have an "oceanic experience" of mystical oneness with the universe while at the breast—and many psychiatrists not dogmatically committed to Freudian theory continue to report clinical evidence that they do—then this was also true among our hairy ancestors crouching around campfires in the dawn of history. If we continue to seek this experience in adult life, then so did they.

But this conclusion leads to results that few of us have ever thought about. According to David Cole Gordon's brilliant study of masturbation, *Self-Love*, the search for adult "oceanic experiences" includes such diverse behaviors as all forms of sex, gambling, watching football games, certain kinds of crime, religious mysticism, mountain climbing and even stud poker. In each of these, the person seeks to plunge into an ocean of sensation so intensely involving and pleasurable that the usual barrier between Self and World is forgotten or totally transcended. Obviously, many kinds of work—if self-chosen and deeply meaningful—also fall into the oceanic category (one thinks of scientific research, literature, art, music, etc.). So does every variety of play or game, and especially contests in which fear is deliberately faced and transcended, such as auto racing or bullfighting. But once we have traced the oceanic experience this far, it is hard to see where we can draw the line at all, except at necessity itself—i.e., that which the universe forces us to do in order to survive. Everything else—everything that is part of the fabric of "culture" or human imagination rather than just given to us by nature—seems to have this element of seeking blissful transcendence. An Ernest Hemingway getting his oceanic sensations by standing firm and firing his rifle at a charging lion; a student transported and carried out of himself or herself by the singing of "We Shall Not Be Moved" (and the shared fear of the cops) at a protest demonstration; a compulsive bank-robber feeling his adrenaline jump as he walks into a heavily guarded treasury with no more than his own brains and bravery to carry him through; the researcher in the seventeenth hour of a test run, having lost all track of self, time, food, friends and everything except the data being recorded; little Portnoy ecstatically masturbating over his sister's brassiere; the intrepid yogi who has held the same *asana* (posture) for ten hours while endlessly repeating the *mantra* "Hare Krishna"; the bridge-builder and bullfighter and the poet finding his rhyme—all of them, are, in a very profound biological sense, repeating or seeking to repeat a state of consciousness first learned at the breast.

And it is only because people have been doing such weird things since the dawn of history that there *is* history at all; otherwise we would be as changeless and stereotyped as all the other mammals. The breast quest, in a thousand million sublimated or generalized forms, is the essence of that restless searching which makes us human.

Because, dig, man, when Mallory was asked why he had to climb Everest and he gave his classic Zen answer, "Because it's there," he was only telling part of the truth; and the other part is well known to all readers of Freud. And we can guess why Aleister Crowley, the poet who devoted so much of his life to the attempt to replace the Father God, Jehovah, with the ancient Egyptian Mother Goddess, Nuit, was also a dedicated mountain climber—the best in England in his day. The force that sends men hurtling through the gravityless vacuum of interplanetary space, risking the most truly *cosmic* terrors in all human history—do we need to ask why, or wonder at the entranced sound in their voices when they radio back to us and speak of the "peace" and "beauty" they have found? The moon—*la luna*—is female in almost all languages and identified with the mother goddess in almost all mythologies. The great artists? We don't have to look at their nudes for evidence: Turn to the paintings without human figures in them and study the logic of line itself—what form appears most often? And what of the musicians? Well, where did you hear music first, who hummed or sang it to you, and against what portion of her body were you being held? The architects break away from the structural necessity of the engineering straight line whenever they can to introduce a softening curve which unconsciously reminds us of—*what*? As for our eating and drinking utensils, do they not attempt to remind us always of our first nourishment? And the great Aristotle himself recorded the significant debate about esthetics occurring in his own day; to wit:

> The Pythagoreans are of the opinion that the shapes of the Greek vases are reflections of the irrational numbers thought by the Pure Mind. On the other hand, the Epicureans hold them to be derived from the curves of a girl's breasts and thighs and buttocks.

---

[1] Timothy Leary, Ph.D., and a few other psychedelic heretics have claimed that imprinting can be removed if the counterconditioning is given while the subject is on an LSD trip. This has not been confirmed, since the government has prevented further research in this field since 1967.

[2] Weston La Barre, *The Ghost Dance: Origins of Religion* (New York: Dell Publishing Company, 1972).

2. Tales of the vienna woods

. . .but we grisly old Sykos who have done our unsmiling bit on alices, when they were yung and easily freudened . . .
—Joyce, *Finnegans Wake.*

According to folklore, two psychoanalysts met on the street one morning. "Good day," said the first politely. The other nodded and walked on. A block later he stopped in his tracks and said aloud, "Now I wonder what he was trying to hide?"

Yes, cousin, psychoanalysts do carry the tendency to seek hidden meanings so far that they often appear absurd to the rest of us, simple and open souls that we are. First the Freudians found symbolism in dreams—and we'll buy that: a long tradition says these psychedelic night-visitors carry messages. Then they found meaning in slips of the tongue, and everybody who remembers Richard Milhous Nixon saying "This nation can't stand Pat" knows that even the most artful dodger occasionally blurts out a home truth. (I once even heard the brilliant Malcolm X stumble and reveal, then quickly conceal, the worst thing we have done to our black citizens, saying, "And I hate every drop of bla—I mean, *white* blood in my veins!")

The Freudians then went on to find hidden meanings in art and literature, and most creative types will admit that their inspiration comes up from a depth imperfectly understood: Faulkner says his novels were dictated by "the Demon;" Mailer speaks of "The Navigator in the Unconscious;" Blake thought the Archangel Gabriel was telling him what to write and paint. Encouraged, the analysts went on to find similar coded symbols in religion, mythology, folklore, in science itself, in all the products of the human imagination.

Eventually, Norman O. Brown was soberly writing that every sentence is a symbolic coitus, the subject being male, the object female and the verb acting as penis. Somewhere along the line Freudianism had passed from science to theology and found itself the proud possessor of a system that explains everything.

A panchreston—an idea that explains everything—is the logical equivalent of a panacea—a medicine that cures everything—or of the perpetual-motion machine in physics. Such ideals cannot possibly exist. We all know this intuitively, if we have any common sense at all, and Russell and Whitehead, with a strange passion for proving the obvious, have demonstrated it at length in their *Principia Mathematica*. A human formula which explains all human formulas is technically in "the class of all classes which include themselves" and leads to logical contradictions. It is therefore invalid in logic and mathematics. Good: We thus dispose of the more grandiose Freudians, and get rid of Thomas Aquinas, Marx, Ayn Rand and other absolutists for good measure. We are also free of that damned barber who shaves every man who doesn't shave himself, in the old riddle. (If he shaves himself, he violates the definition, but if he doesn't shave himself he also violates the definition. When we realize that he belongs to the logically invalid "class of all classes that include themselves" we are through with him forever.)

So: however hard the Freudians drive us, there is one sanctuary to which we can flee. They literally cannot explain everything. Somewhere there is a door they cannot force, a temple they cannot enter, a logically necessary refuge which their panchreston cannot incorporate, and there we can still maintain our mysterious and dreadful freedom.

It has to be admitted though, that outside the last bastion Freud and his satraps have explained a great deal—in fact, more than most people cared to have had explained. A man who is fastidiously neat, careful about balancing his budget, eager to take an authoritarian role and give orders to others—an ideal businessman type in short—is probably an *anal* personality. His whole psychic economy is involved with symbolic substitutes for the struggles of will that went on in infancy during toilet training. Bankers, accountants and mathematicians, as well as businessmen, are often of this type. An uncomfortable thought? Then there's the compulsively, chronically, monotonously promiscuous fellow— guess what? He's probably a repressed homosexual. Each woman drives him away quickly by her femininity; each new woman is grabbed just as rapidly to stave off his unconscious desire for another man. Does the shoe pinch yet? Then there's the gentle soul, the liberal, the bleeding heart who cares for all people and suffers every pain in the universe as if it were his own. He's an *oral* personality, still symbolically nursing at the breast.

Of course, nothing is quite as simple as these labels would lead one to believe. Few of us are *nothing more* than one of these Freudian categories, except in the literary or dramatic arts where writers can simplify for dramatic effect. Purely oral types—Chekhov's Uncle Vanya, Joyce's Leopold Bloom, the timid little guys played by Danny Kaye, Harold Lloyd, Wally Cox or Dennis Hopper—would probably not survive to adulthood in the real world.

Nevertheless, there are statistical clusters that remain fairly consistent in psychological testing, and have repeatedly been confirmed during several decades of such probing. Given 300 verbal statements to mark "I agree" or "I disagree," certain men will agree with most of the statements consistent with an oral personality—that is, a personality largely determined by conditioning and imprinting received during the nursing stage and therefore oriented chiefly toward a mother archetype. Other men will agree with most of the statements consistent with an anal personality—a personality largely determined by conditioning and imprinting received during toilet training or other early conflicts with social rules of "morality" or "decorum."

For instance, the statement "I hate to see some smart lawyer bedazzle a jury and get some no-good criminal off scot-free"—which you must have seen on one of these personality quizzes at some time in your college or business career—is always rejected by a purely oral type, who will check "I disagree," and accepted by a purely anal type, who will check "I agree." This is because the oral type identifies with the underdog in every situation and assumes that the defendant is accused wrongly or got into trouble through no fault of his own. Anal types, on the other hand, have "introjected" the father archetype or authority principle, and are always looking for somebody to punish[3].

Interestingly enough, if you take the same group and give them a nonverbal test such as the TAT (Thematic Apperception Test), in which they look at pictures and make up stories about them, the oral types will devise oral stories, the anal types will project anal stories, introverts and extroverts will see characteristically introverted or extroverted situations, etc., thereby illustrating the dictum of the first great psychologist, Buddha—that the world we see is our own fantasy. For instance, one standard picture shows a young man facing an old lady who has a sad expression. To the oral type, they are mother and son, he has done wrong, but she is about to forgive him; to an anal type, however, he is more likely to be a bill collector, she is trying to con him by crying, but he'll get the money anyhow. . . .

Before following these Freudian concepts any further, let us stop to look at a historical incident which seems apropos. Freckle-faced Phryne, the most famous of the courtesans of Athens in the 4th Century B.C., was approximately contemporary with Pericles, Socrates, Alcibiades, Aristophanes and Plato—a lively group of conversationalists, to say the least. They had other colorful traits, too: Alcibiades, one of the best generals of his time, was probably the homosexual lover of Socrates (who had a wife and a mistress on the side), and was once disgraced and sent into exile for a drunken prank in which he cut the penises off the statues of various gods in the city. Phryne herself was not only lovely (they say she posed for some of Praxiteles's voluptuous goddesses) but something of an independent thinker herself, like most of the well-educated and artistically talented courtesan class. (Athenian wives, on the other hand, were encouraged to remain both stupid and submissive. Among its other glories and abominations, Athens evidently pioneered what Women's Lib now calls male chauvinism.)

Phryne eventually got into serious trouble for her ideas and was accused of impiety and disrespect for the gods; this was a capital offense and Socrates later died for it. In Phryne's case the court also seemed inclined to take a harsh view—just a while before, they had sent Anaxagoras into exile for saying that the way he figured it, the sun probably wasn't a god at all but just a big hunk of burning rock. Seeing that things were going against her, Phryne (or her lawyer; accounts differ) pulled down her robe, exposed her fair bosom to the judges and said this was her testimony. She was acquitted.

Cynics will say the judges were horny old men. Esthetes generally interpret the story as a noble illustration of the religious awe that the Athenians had for beauty. Phryne had said, in effect, does this vision not prove the gods are pleased with me? Since the act of baring the breast was a traditional sign of worship among the female devotees of the great mother goddess, it is possible that Phryne was, indeed, testifying to her piety; see our discussions later of the breast repressed and unrepressed. A very ingenious Freudian, however, might offer a more psychological interpretation.

Judges, according to Freudian theory, tend to be very anal individuals, but being human they must have some oral component and a trace of tenderness and forgiveness. Phryne's dramatic gesture, whether or not it reminded them of the rites of the great goddess (at that point in decline, being replaced by those of the father god, Zeus, but still practiced at least yearly at the Eleusinian Mysteries), almost

certainly startled them into oral memories and associations. . . .
It might almost be considered an early example of Action or
Gestalt therapy. Similar partial or total nudity is used by the
more radical Encounter therapists to jar people back into
awareness of primordial realities underlying our cruel and
complicated social games of reward and punishment.

(See Dicken's astonishing use of the nude female breast
as a reminder of all we have lost in this cruel civilization, in
the passage from *David Copperfield* to be quoted later. I also
recall Josef von Sternberg's *Marked Woman*, which has the
most painful climax in cinema history: Marlene Dietrich,
about to be shot by a firing squad, asks for a mirror and
comb in order to fix her hair before dying. These are provided, and she holds the mirror to her face and raises the
comb to her hair; the gesture is so beautifully and delicately
feminine that one soldier bursts into tears, throws down his
rifle and refuses to shoot. He is led off in disgrace and a man
better adjusted to our civilization takes his place. She is
shot—and the audience comes out with the most ghastly
silence you have ever heard in a movie theater. Nobody
looks at anybody else in the lobby.)

Returning to our oral and anal types: After we have
identified them through the verbal tests and that TAT, some
interesting things happen if we put them in a group therapy
session. The anal types will immediately try to dominate the
therapist, or, failing that, they will try to compete with him
for authority over the rest of the group. The oral types, on
the other hand, will quickly broadcast how helpless they are
and how much care they need. This is so commonplace that
the therapist, without seeing the previous test results at all
and without time for a real "depth analysis," will still classify
them into these groups, precisely as the man marking the
tests has classified them. (This experiment has been tried
repeatedly, with the results as predicted by Freudian theory.
Dr. Timothy Leary, of LSD fame, was one of the first to set
up a large-scale experiment of this sort. Curiously, his own

testing procedures were used on him a decade later when he entered prison.)

But if this much of Freudian theory is true—if most people will show the same tendencies in their verbal responses, their visual imagination and their actual behavior in groups—we had better look a bit more closely at the good doctor Freud's ideas about breast and oralism. At least, that might tell us why this book turns us on (and why many of us feel secretly guilty about being turned on by it).

The pleasure of the child at the breast, says Freud, is sexual pleasure. The love of the child for its mother is sexual love. This does not mean that the little boy wants to possess his mother in the manner of adult sexuality or that the little girl is necessarily a little lesbian. It means that the basic physical and psychological bliss is, on an energetic and biological level, the same that we later experience in adult sexuality. Two Freudian revisionists, Wilhelm Reich, M.D., and Frederick Perls, M.D., Ph.D., have clarified this somewhat by pointing out that *anxiety* is also the same energy running in the opposite direction. Let us call it excitement, to be simple. When excitement is aroused, when energy seeks an outlet in action, one either goes forward to the goal (energy discharge) or one blocks and hesitates. In any discharge, the same energetic processes are occurring, and this is what Freud means in saying all pleasure is sexual pleasure. If there is a block, the same energy annoyingly remains "on tap" as it were, and this sensation is called anxiety. On the verbal level, this state is expressed by such phrases as "Oh, I don't know what to do—I'm afraid—Either choice seems equally bad." Freud called this *Besetzung*, which in German has the primal meaning of sitting down. Brill, Freud's American translator, turned this into the more academic-looking *cathexis*, which is a two-dollar Latin word that on etymological examination turns out to mean the same as sitting down. Reich called it "emotional anchoring," which is more poetic and suggests a ship being held back by a heavy weight, while Perls, with typical earthiness, just calls it *being stuck*.

Thus, there is nothing wrong with the infant's bliss at the breast; it is entirely appropriate for that age. There is nothing wrong with the personality and behaviors he develops to enjoy that stage to its utmost. *Barring emotional shocks or other environmental attacks on him,* he will grow easily and naturally into other stages, keeping just as much of this love-sex experience as continues to be useful and appropriate. That is, he will always have an oral element, but it will not be the perimeter and boundary line of his personality and behavior; it will just be one part.

This oral element has many delightful and beneficent functions in later life. It makes us love women's breast, kiss them, cuddle them, suck them, play with them. It makes us love pictures of women's breasts. (Hence, prudes and women's liberationists will never get rid if such "pornographic" or "chauvinistic" art until they first find some way to get rid of the neoteny—the prolonged infancy—of the human species. Even bottle-fed infants acquire oralism, since the bottle remains stubbornly a *dead* breast substitute but still a *breast substitute*.) The oral element also makes it possible, if we are lucky, to experience the "oceanic consciousness" of the mystics, for, if Freud is right, this is a development of the union-with-mother that the nursing child feels. It also gives us what share we have in warmth, kindness, generosity and that very oral virtue, forgiveness. In short, if we have any tenderness at all, we haven't fully repressed our oral element.

It should be obvious at this point that the historical Yeshua of Nazareth (the Jesus Christ of Christian mythology) was a man with a considerable oral element. He had a high degree of mystic oneness with the universe. He loved little children and compared them to the kingdom of heaven. He sympathized with publicans and sinners. He even forgave those who crucified him. It is not surprising that so many artists have intuitively portrayed him as a small infant nursing at the breast of Mary. His is a totally oral religion. Part of the confusing and schizophrenic quality of American life is the result of an official allegiance to this religion combined with an economic system of cutthroat capitalism, which is based on a totally anal rejection of all these tender oral values. Only the admixture of anality in Christianity itself, deposited by the legalistic woman-hater St. Paul, allows the incompatible mixture to come off at all.

Orality becomes sick and sinister when the person is *cathected* or *stuck* at that psychological stage and cannot or will not develop the personality traits of later childhood and maturity. The cathected oral personality carries forgiveness much further than Jesus himself—who, after all, was capable of shouting angry denunciations at the "generation of vipers" around him, condemning lawyers as "hypocrites" and even taking a whip to the usurious money changers in the temple. In Dr. Perl's striking terminology, the mature person makes *demands* on others and on the world, but the oral personality only harbors *resentments*. Look hard and unflinchingly at something or somebody you resent, and there you will find a trace of pathological oralism in you. The healthy process, confronted by frustration, is to tell the frustrator to get the hell out of your way. The oral process is to submit, forgive the frustrator for his primitive and insensitive nature (so much less "spiritual" than the oralist himself) and then to harbor an unspoken resentment.

As Dr. Perls has written:

> If you have any difficulties in communication with anyone, look for your resentments. Resentments are among the worst possible unfinished situations—unfinished gestalts. If you resent, you can neither let go nor have it out. Resentment is an emotion of central importance. The resentment is the most important expression of an impasse—of being stuck. If you feel resentment, be able to express your resentment. A resentment unexpressed often is experienced as, or changes into, feelings of guilt. Whenever you feel guilty, find out what you

are resenting and express it and make your demands explicit.
This alone will help a lot[4].

The dependent and resentful oral personality programs
his life around a technique which actor-director Mike Nichols
once called "winning by losing." In any conflict, we can
wither win boldly and frankly by winning—or we can win
symbolically by losing. That is, if we have the classic oral
rationalizations, we can convince ourselves that our loss was
a spiritual or moral victory. It showed our superiority to the
crude and bullying rascal whom we graciously refused to
fight directly. If you watch people who are especially good
at this technique, you will see that they always convey the
resentment-filled message that they are the real winners,
either by tone of voice or by posture and "body language" or
through some other subtle form of nonverbal communication.

An old cartoon shows a top sergeant shouting at a
recruit: "And wipe that opinion off your face!" The rookie,
unable to win against the army system in any ordinary way,
was evidently regressing to his oral component and trying
to signal that he was still winning—by losing.

The cathected oral personality attempts to turn all human relations into a series of encounters with an enormous,
rounded, firmly nippled, all-providing pair of breasts. If you
can't or won't play that role, he then turns you into an
avatar of the "denying mother" or "bad mother" (Freud's
terms), who selfishly and malignantly withholds the treas-
ured nipples. Of course, if you like being a pair of nipples,
there is a fortune to be made—just acquire a psychiatrist's
license and go into business. These types will be glad to pay
your fees, whatever they are, not only for years, but even
for decades. There is only one rule: Never try to be a true
psychiatrist—never try to cure them—or they will become
disillusioned and seek another therapist, another symbolic
wet nurse.

"I can't bear listening to all this misery day after day,"

one psychiatrist complains to another, in an old joke. "So, who listens?" says the second.

The fact is that the majority of people in psychotherapy at a given moment are likely to be pure oral types or to have a large oral element mixed with other traits. This is because the oralist enters every situation seeking help from somebody else, and the psychiatrist seems to offer the kind of help that is most needed—mothering. On the other hand, the opposite extreme, the totally anal personality, is hardly ever found in psychotherapy. *This is because he is seldom miserable himself;* he just makes everybody around him miserable. For no matter how you try to relate to an anal type—no matter how carefully you study his power game and try to predict his rules—it always turns out that you are at least slightly wrong and need some measure of correction from his inexhaustible fount of moral superiority.

(The superficially "rational" and well-adjusted anal types become business executives or judges, as we have said. They also infest mathematics, banking, accounting, professorships in the "hard" or "exact" sciences, atomic research and the military. The often-repeated Freudian comment that ours is an anal culture merely means that it has many power and prestige positions which are attractive to anal types, who thereupon muscle into those positions and then have the socially defined authority to inflict their own anal values on everybody else. These characteristic anal values—as contrasted to the childish dependency, emotional warmth, kindness, generosity, forgiveness, buried resentment and pervasive "Uncle Tom" masochism or "Good Soldier Schweik" incompetence of the oral type—are efficiency, precision, hatred of the body and of all mess or dirt, fear of emotional contact, stern realism and moralistic desire to meddle in everybody else's life. The more hysterical and less rational anal types tend to become policemen or collectors of bad debts for credit corporations.)

The shock and dismay of the infant when the harshness

of traditional toilet training introduces the anal-rational-moral values into the previously cozy oral-oceanic state is conveyed with remarkable overt symbolism in Charles Dicken's *David Copperfield*. So Freudian is this sequence, indeed that it is hard to believe that it was actually written half a century before Freud defined the oral and anal stages in his *Three Contributions to the Theory of Sex*.

Dickens describes an idyllic childhood in which David lives with a widowed mother who can safely be categorized as a secular version of the *bona dea* (good goddess) of the ancients. Onto this happy scene intrudes the horrible Mr. Murdstone, whose "Jehovah complex" (as any modern psychiatrist would call it) makes him an avatar of the archetypal punishing father god. There is no way of obeying all of Murdstone's rules; there are too many of them and most of them are unstated and implicit anyway. David undergoes some monumental lashings on the buttocks (for his own good, of course, although Dickens emphasizes in a quite Freudian way the obvious enjoyment Mr. Murdstone obtains from these sessions). Quite naturally, David begins to internalize this anal system of values (especially after Murdstone becomes his stepfather) and imagines that he is quite a guilty little wretch and richly deserves this torture. Then—in a quite eerie echo of Phryne or of Eleanor of Aquitaine baring her breasts in Jerusalem at the height of the medieval patriarchal age—Dickens has the following scene, when David returns from a year at school:

> I went in with quiet, timid step.
>
> God knows how infantine the memory may have been that was awakened in me at the sound of my mother's voice in the old parlour when I set foot in the hall. I think I must have laid in her arms and heard her singing to me when I was a baby. The strain was new to me but it was so old that it filled my heart brimful like a friend come back form a long absense.
>
> I believed from the solitary and thoughtful way in which my mother murmered her song that she was alone, and I

went softly into the room. She was sitting by the fire, suckling an infant whose tiny hand she held against her neck. Her eyes were looking down upon its face and she sat singing to it. I was so far right that she had no other companion. I spoke to her and she started and cried out. But seeing me she called me her dear Davy, her own boy! and coming half way across the room to meet me, kneeled down upon the ground and kissed me, and laid my head down on her bosom near the little creature that was nestling there, and put its hand up to my lips.

I wish I had died. I wish I had died then, with that feeling in my heart. I should have been more fit for heaven than I have ever been since.

It is normal at present to squirm with embarrassment at Dickens's sentimentality, just as it was normal to squirm with embarrassment (or prurience) at what was an equally eloquent sex scene back in the days when *he* was writing. And yet—if one can put aside ones's resentment at the very obvious ways he is playing on the reader's heartstrings—the only intelligent response to this scene is frank admiration for the man's insight. The return to the mother's breast to escape the harsh "morality" of the punishing father or father god is a tendency so strong that it has been recognized not only by Freud but by the overwhelming majority of Freud's revisionists. Unless we understand that part of us is still seeking this whenever we caress a woman's so-called secondary sex zones in the breasts, we will be making love in a psychological darkness as neurotic as the physical darkness which our grandparents imposed on their bedrooms.

Of course, Murdstone is soon back on the scene again and David undergoes further miseries. A Catholic bishop once complained that Jane Russell's breasts hung "like a storm cloud" over every scene in *the Outlaw*; David's mother's breasts hang like the sun itself over the growing darkness of the Murdstone world until David finally frees himself from it by becoming Charles Dickens and denouncing the cruelty, hypocrisy and scarcely sublimated sadism that made up the Victorian theory of child-rearing.

It is amusing to note (although this could hardly be conscious on Dickens's part), that the last syllable of Mr. Murdstone's name suggests the hard, rocky impression that anal types usually convey, while the first syllable is suggestive of the French *merde*, excrement.

Dickens's ability to communicate movingly how insanely cruel Murdstone's child-rearing methods seem to the child himself eventually resulted in widespread liberalization and Dr. Spock. The same result, however, is still achieved by more subtle psychological conditioning in all but the most "progressive" families; David Copperfield's story is still moving because we have all passed through something like it. We do not bring the oral bliss with us, as Jesus evidently did, into adulthood; it is always disrupted by an anal-moralistic period. This is why the oral types we encounter are not carrying their infantile traits as graciously and benevolently as Jesus *and do not seem like second Christs but like caricatured Christs*. They are carrying their orality resentfully, spitefully and neurotically, not integrating it into an adult realism, but using it to stave off maturity. This is the stubborn quality of the neurotic which Freud called *Besetzung* or *Cathexis*.

But, of course, all oral traits in adulthood are not necessarily neurotic. It has been said that the happiest man is he who has forgiven most (and only those who have truly learned how to forgive can understand that statement); but there would be no forgiveness without some oral remnant in the personality. The totally anal person never forgives anything—which may explain why the conservatives, who are always anal, have chosen the elephant, symbol of long memory, as their symbol.

Orality also adds a great deal to sex. (It is perhaps an indication of the strength of my own oral component that I cannot imagine a totally anal person, who never performs orally, being a satisfactory sexual partner[5].) As Freud pointed out, orality has not only extended downward from the breasts but upward as well, and the mouth-to-mouth kiss—which is what we usually mean when we just say "the kiss"—is its most astonishing manifestation. In fact, behind Freud's ponderous Germanic-scientific style in *Three Contributions to the Theory of Sex*, he sounds rather amused at the fact that mouth-mouth contact was *not* considered a perversion while, in his time, mouth-genital contact emphatically was. After all, if we try to argue that genital-genital coupling is ordained by God as the one permissible diversion for earth people, then mouth-genital pleasures are only *one* step away from the "norm" while mouth-mouth kissing is *two* steps away and thus doubly perverted. As for nibbling the earlobes . . .!

Freud also points out that there is something irrational in the commonplace reaction that causes a man to feel revulsion if he accidentally uses a woman's toothbrush although he may have been kissing her rapturously just a short while earlier[6].

It was Kinsey, two generations later, who pointed out the similar irrationality of those who experience revulsion at the thought of cunnilingus or fellatio because "germs might be transmitted." Germs, the no-nonsense Indiana zoologist commented sternly, are much more likely to be transmitted by mouth-to-mouth kissing.

In fact, as Freud was aware, all alleged "reasons" for rejecting orality are rationalizations. One is afraid or repulsed by the thought of such acts because one has been trained to be afraid or repulsed, and all the "reasons" are invented later. (Flaubert once commented on middle-class young men who avoid prostitutes because of fear of venereal disease "and then catch the most beautiful cases of clap from their sweethearts.") In fact, revulsion against any pleasurable act is a mark of terrors left in the psyche by some anal figure in early life—a parent, uncle, aunt, older brother, teacher, etc. There is a hilarious essay—or a whole book—on the reasons people give for not trying marijuana or for staying in jobs or mar friages that they hate, or for obeying obviously idiotic and unenforceable laws, etc. In most cases, except where real harm to innocent individuals is probable, our fears are entirely phobic and absurd. Just as an old college song reduces all the problems of ontology to Zenlike empiricism—

> We're here because we're here,
> because we're here, because we're here . . .

—it is equally true, almost always, to say that

> We're scared because we're scared,
> because we're scared, because we're scared . . .

Fortunately, the fears that infest below-the-belt orality have not seriously infected the breast quest itself. I did read once, however, in some Dear Crabby—or Ann Launders— column, about a woman who was afraid of allowing her husband too much gratification of that sort for fear it might give her breast cancer. In such a case, one hardly needs Freud to see that the ostensible "reason" for the fear was created after the fear itself. The really significant form of repression of orality in our culture is the phobia against breast-feeding infants, which began in the 1920s, peaked in the 1950s and has been declining (very slowly) ever since. but this subject, which may relate to the paranoid trend of our society generally, will be treated in the chapter "The Breast Repressed."

Freudianism itself reached some kind of climax or peak during those same years with the remarkable career of Edmund Bergler, M.D. Dr. Bergler became convinced that not some but *all* human neuroses were caused by desire for the breast— but in a very peculiar sense. The oneness of the infant at the nipple, he said, was literally believed by the infant, and the fundamental trauma of life was the shocked discovery that this wonderful object belonged to somebody else—to mother. Worse yet, she could withhold it on occasion. From this, Dr. Bergler claimed, there came a desire for revenge which was the secret core of every subsequent action.

This, of course, is no odder sounding than most Freudian theories, but Dr. Bergler was just beginning. His theories became increasingly imaginative and all-inclusive. In *Money and the Unconscious*, he proved that every patient who ever had trouble meeting his high fees was actually withholding the money to punish him for being right. In *Fashion and the Unconscious*, he proved—and this has always been my favorite—that women's clothes are all hideously ugly because they are designed by homosexuals seeking revenge against their mothers for withholding the breast, and are accepted by women because they, poor dears, are all masochists secretly devoted to punishing themselves. In *Neurotic Counterfeit Sex*, he proved that everything Kinsey found statistically normal is actually neurotic and that only the "missionary position" (as the Hawaiians call man-on-top coitus) is normal. In *Writers and the Unconscious*, he proved that everybody who has ever written a book was a repressed homosexual, chewing and sucking on words as "regular" homosexuals chew and suck on penises, as substitutes for the denied breast. In between these remarkable tomes, he wrote endless articles proving that all critics of his theories—who by then were legion in psychoanalytical and psychiatric circles—were neurotic. He eventually became the favorite hate-object of the Gay Liberation Front and it is as such that he is remembered, which is really a pity because some of his notions were probably at least partially true.

Finally, Ira Wallach, in a book that appeared to be satire, *Hopalong Freud Rides Again*, suggested that just as every woman wishes to have a penis (according to the Master), every man wishes to have a pair of breasts. Was this really parody? Carl Jung, the most prestigious of Freud's rivals, argues soberly that each sex unconsciously wishes to become more like the other and that this desire finds increasing expression with age—as proofs of which he offered the mustaches on old women and the pendulous breasts on old men. Again, are we sure he is completely wrong? The universal human experience of prolonged infancy has conditioned and imprinted us in so many ways that any speculation about the breast is, at very least, a fantasy that has occurred to more than one mind in history and is thus part of our human heritage.

There is, for instance, the puzzling phenomenon of oral sadism. On a simple reading of Freud's original theories, this should not exist at all, since only the calamities of toilet training produce the reactive sadism of the anal types. (*Petard*, the old word for bomb, comes from the same root as *fart*, and the military mentality can be defined as the search for a satisfactorily orgasmic superexplosion which leaves everybody dead, like the epic farts in certain jokes.) According to Freud, who may be a bit imaginative here, oral sadism, on the other hand, derives from the infant's cannibalistic fantasies while at the breast. (We adults still say, "I could eat you all up" when transported by erotic bliss.) This theme is characteristic of the werewolf and vampire legends which have been around at least since the New Stone Age and received a new currency when Hollywood discovered their commercial appeal in the 1930's.

One could hazard a guess that there is not a child in America—or in any country where Hollywood films circulate—who is not familiar with the whole grisly lore of how a man bitten by the werewolf becomes a werewolf, how these creatures are seized at the full moon (sign of the mother goddess) with the lust for human flesh, and how that other jolly fellow, the vampire, rises from the grave to suck blood from the living. Ernest Jones wrote the first psychoanalytic study of this legendry back in 1910, even before Hollywood discovered it, and pointed out the ambivalence and strange sympathy these monsters evoke—a compassionate identification rationalized by the thought, "They can't help what they've become," a notion seldom remembered about our human enemies in wartime (or any other time for that matter). The fact is that we not only identify masochistically with their victims but also identify sadistically with the monsters themselves—which can be seen very clearly in young children.

These oral monsters represent impulses which, in any oral sex act, are close to the surface but carefully repressed either because of taboo or loving empathy with the other party. Thus, we only *say* "I could eat you all up" but content ourselves with licking, kissing and gentle nibbling. Gershon Legman suggests that male contempt for a lady who is overly enthusiastic about fellatio—"She's *just* a cocksucker" a fellow will say, after having enjoyed her company for precisely that reason—derives from more than the antihedonistic bias of Christian culture. Legman thinks there is an unconscious fear that this impulse can go too far and become real oral sadism. Similarly, many women seem to indulge male orality largely out of a sense that the man needs to think he's a great and skillful lover—perhaps they could enjoy it more if not bothered by unacknowledged fears that he might go off his head and actually start chewing and ripping. Oral sex notoriously gets better as the partners live together longer and learn to trust each other more totally.

In this connection, an anecdote in Legman's *The Rationale of the Dirty Joke* is apropos. One embittered woman, who had probably known too many male chauvinists in her life, developed a singularly oral-sadistic revenge. She would lure married men to her apartment, fellate them while they were still dressed, then spit the semen onto their trousers and say, "Explain that to your wife, you son of a bitch!" One gentleman, a professor, hearing of this, allowed himself to be led into her trap. When she was finished with her performance, he calmly arose, removed his trousers, took another pair from his briefcase, put them on, tipped his hat and left.

It is anal squeamishness about orality, of course, which has made "sucks" into a very, very dirty word, immortalized in the common graffiti informing the world that "Tom sucks" or "Suzie sucks" or "Policemen suck" and so forth. In the 1960s, this became politicized, and graffiti saying "Johnson sucks" appeared wherever radicals congregated. Norman Mailer even tells of seeing "Pentagon sucks" written on the wall of the Pentagon itself during the huge antiwar demonstration there in 1967, and he comments that even if soldiers usually dislike pacifists, the lower ranks would enjoy that particular expression of pacifist sentiment. The elaboration, "The army is like a joint[7]—the more you suck, the higher you get," now appears in latrines everywhere.

Eventually, the politics of suck gave birth to parodies, of which the most memorable was "Dracula sucks." Interestingly, the growing public awareness of Freudianism implied in that joke was also mirrored in the horror films of the 1960s, in which the vampires became increasingly sexy and the neck bite was quite often very sensuously treated; most notable was Roger Vadim's sophisticated and decadent *Blood and Roses*. The strange sensibility of Roman Polansky finally took the logical step, and in a campy horror-comedy, *The Fearless Vampire-Killers, or Pardon Me, But Your Teeth Are In My Neck*, the vampire had a son who was an explicit phatic homosexual of the exhibitionistic "screaming faggot" variety. (Another vampire in the same movie was Jewish and refused to be frightened away by the traditional crucifix.) Of course, Bela Lugosi had understood Freud well enough in his own way, and his classic *Dracula*, directed by Tod Browning, suggests perverse sexuality in dozens of implicit and subliminal ways[8].

The latest graffiti, also available as a lapel button, reduces the whole negative connotation of "suck" to absurdity by informing us, with simple biological truth, "Babies suck."

---

[3] See my notes on our anal cuss-words *ass, ass-hole, shit* and *pig* in Robert Anton Wilson, *Playboy's Book of Forbidden Words*(New York: Playboy Press, 1972).

[4] Frederick Perls, *Gestalt Therapy Verbatim* (New York: Bantam Books, 1971).

[5] I actually scored higher on anality in a standard psychological test—but not *much* higher.

[6] In another place he mentions that the normal or average revulsion against the use of the anus in sexual intercourse because it is "contaminated" by the passage of feces is exactly similar to the claim of some hysterical female patients that they can't accept the penis because it is used for the passage of urine. The implication was too daring even for him, and he quickly adds that he is not "espousing the cause" of the homosexuals.

[7] A marijuana cigarette.

[8] Readers interested in the sociology and psychology of the werewolf legend should see my article, "'Even a Man Who Is Pure Of Heart': The American Horror Film As Folk-Art," in *Journal of Human Relations*, Summer 1970.

3. The breast repressed

The young men ("brothers"), long-haired and bearded, were hoeing the field. A few young women ("sisters") worked alongside them. One sister, wearing a dress with a loose-fitting top, bent over and inadvertently allowed a brother to glimpse her breasts. Later in the day a brother complained to a pastor that the sister had "stumbled" him—she had caused him to have fleshly desires. . . . . That evening after dinner the sisters had a special meeting. . . . . Sisters who were "older in the Lord" explained that it was necessary for women to dress in a manner that revealed neither ankle nor curve.[9]

—"Jesus People"

It's the truth I'm telling you: This is not a report on a medieval fiefdom visited with the first time-machine. This is a commune of "Jesus Freaks" existing in the United States today, in the decade following the first moon-walk, a century after Charles Darwin, 300 years after Galileo. And yet it is not without precedent. In the 1920's our whole society went through a phase of trying to conceal or eliminate the female breast; and even worse happened in the Dark Ages, both to the breast and to the rest of the unfortunate female.

Psychologically, the roots of this mammalophobia are easily found. Freud's "anal personality" (the "authoritarian personality" in the more sociological, less biological, psychology of Erich Fromm) is conditioned or imprinted by early experiences of shame about his excremental functions. He develops secondary queasiness about all other unconditioned or primordial body eruptions including sexual passion, unrestrained joy of any sort, loud laughter, tears, the mammal habit of cuddling (whether in puppies, kittens, children or adult lovers) and spontaneous rage. (His is rather an icy "intellectual" anger and the kind of revenge Poe described in *The Cask of Amontillado*.) Most of all, he rejects the homeostatic functions of the body's servomechanism system (Fuller's "Phantom Captain"), especially excretion itself, then urination, masturbation, the visible symptoms of pregnancy and, of course, lactation. Extreme anal types are notorious for their food phobias and can't stand milk, tapioca pudding, creamed vegetables or anything else that reminds them of their own oral stage in infancy.

The strength of the anal component in our culture, indeed, is demonstrated by the continuing efforts to roll back the advance of sexual frankness in the last decade. Long after it had been made abundantly obvious that the sight of a few nipples would *not* result in the Decline and Fall of the American Empire, the attempt to restore the censorship of the past still finds its powerful allies. In January 1973, the local bluenoses scored a small victory in one of our most wide-open cities, San Francisco. The proprietor of a topless bar who had set up a billboard showing his star attraction revealing her lovely mammaries in all their naked glory was ordered to restore her to a more modest look. He did so, amusingly enough, by plastering a large white strip saying CENSORED across her nipples.

It sometimes appears that Darwin's discoveries are as little understood as Einstein's. The phrase "natural selection", for example, specifically included *sexual selection*, but most people still do not comprehend that this means that humanity is largely its own creation. The male human, for instance, has the largest penis in the primate family; his muscular cousin, the gorilla is, by comparison conspicuously less virile in this respect, contrary to popular lore associated with the fantasy image of the lady carried off by one of these apes. (Average length, flaccid, for the human male, is around 3.7 inches; for the gorilla, two inches. The other primates are closer to the gorilla). While this is not the result of male desire for a long wang in any Christian Science mind-over-matter fashion, it is clearly the result of choices made by female humans and protohumans during our long evolution. The males with longer wangs were selected more often as sexual partners and hence produced more children. Their genes were carried on while the genes of the "pilgrims with shorter muskets" were selectively bred out of the species. The same applies to the female breast, which grew from the flat surface of the female ape to the pleasing cup-shape that we all appreciate so warmly.

Thus, the human body which prudes find so objectionable is the product of human desire, human sexuality and human choices over several million years. If the prudes had dominated for any considerable period, we would probably not be here at all or would be born encased in a concrete overcoat or tortoiseshell through which nobody could ever see or feel.

The anal personality will justify his aversions (which are, of course, actually prompted by anxiety—we are "scared because we're scared, because we're scared, because we're scared . . .") by saying that large naked breasts are "dirty" or "smutty". This, amusingly enough, reveals his own anality; a normally neat woman has no real dirt or smut (from Anglo-Saxon *smotten*, to stain or blacken) on her breasts. Rather, these are *conditioned semantic reactions* in the anal person's own nervous system, generalized expressions of his aversion to bodily parts and processes acquired while his parents were toilet training him. A brief definition of an anal personality in nontechnical terms might be: One who feels for all bodily functions a slightly exaggerated intensification of what normal people feel for turds.

The absurdity of this orientation—the sheer nonsense of identifying a nice, warm, clean, luscious breast with a stinking piece of excrement—is not immediately obvious to us only because it is so commonplace. As fish do not notice the water since it's everywhere in their world, we do not

observe anality as a mental confusion because it is everywhere in our culture. If a man blows his nose in his soup or
claims that Martian invaders are hiding in the broom closet,
we know that his nervous system is not scanning the environment correctly, but if he denounces the things we love
and enjoy most as "filthy and obscene," we are apt to think
he is more spiritual than we are, feel inferior to him and
pretend to agree—at least until we can get away from his
uncomfortable presence.

The same intimidation-by-redundancy or prestige-by-
numbers applies to other delusions. A man today who believed literally the Bible text "Thou shalt not suffer a witch
to live," and sought to revive burning at the stake would be
considered a dangerous lunatic. Similarly, the snake-
handling cult in Georgia and the Carolinas has encountered
some legal harassment over the years, and one of its members was put in a mental hospital, even though their faith is
based on Mark 16:17-18: "And these signs shall follow them
that believe; in my name they shall cast out devils; they shall
speak with new tongues; *they shall take up serpents*; and if
they drink any deadly thing it shall not hurt them." [Italics
mine.] And a Canadian millionaire, two decades ago, was
placed in a mental hospital by his relatives when he accepted
literally, "Take what thou hast and give it to the poor," and
began distributing his wealth to people on the street. Nevertheless, hardly anybody but Madalyn Murray O'Hair dares
to say in public that certain other biblical texts are, by any
rational or objective standard, far madder than these three.
This is because the lunatics who believe such things are, in
this case, the majority and can imprison anyone who disbe-
lieves. Thus, when the Presidential Commission on Pornography and Obscenity concluded that there was no scientific
evidence that sexy literature had ever harmed anyone, President Nixon invoked the great magic word of anal culture,
"smut," and rejected their conclusions. The Nixon-packed
Supreme Court soon followed his example. In the 1980's

President Reagan, convened a new Commission. Rather then risk the embarrassment suffered by President Nixon, Reagan simply stacked the Commission itself, and thus ordained the conclusion: Pornography causes Violence. That the data published by the commission did not support the conclusion is, of course, irrelevant.

In general, anybody who uses the word "smut" cannot be rationally approached on the matter of freedom and censorship, just as anybody who uses the word "nigger" is not likely to listen calmly to the case for Black liberation. Such emotive words carry *conditioned semantic reactions* which involve the whole organism—front brain, lower brain (where emotional processes begin), muscles, glands, guts, the works— and cannot be changed by logic, which reaches the front brain *only*. If logic did control humanity, we all would have achieved perfect sanity when Plato discovered the dialectic of argument and Aristotle published the laws of reasoning. As it is, we are just beginning in this century to discover techniques for removing the phobias and revulsions which keep people effectively blind to much of their environment and the *projections* which they use to cover those realities which cannot be ignored.

As I wrote more than ten years ago in the *Encyclopedia of Sexual Behavior*.

> Sexual attitudes, like other attitudes, generally derive from unspoken and often unconscious premises. Creative thought, which is always articulate and precise, results from frustration: a man sees that a problem must be solved and he creates new thoughts in solving it. But the overwhelming preponderance of human "thought" is not of this purposive, articulate and creative kind. Most of what we consider our mental activity consists of sub-articulate, half-conscious semantic reflexes— reactions to key words as the situation invokes these words in our minds.
>
> For example, our mental reaction to sex—our so-called "philosophy" of sex—is, in most cases, a set of neuropsychological reactions to a few very simple "poetic metaphors." The

particular metaphor that has had the strongest influence on Occidental civilization and that underlies traditional Judeo-Christian sexual dogma is that sex is "dirty." Sexual activity is filthy. Sexual functions are like excremental functions—foul, disgusting, embarrassing, not "nice," etc.

We speak of this as a *simple poetic metaphor* because it can be analyzed as a literary critic analyzes a line of verse. A metaphor is the implicit identification of two different factors. Simile says, "The ship is like a plow." Metaphor, less obvious and therefore more effective, insinuates the identification without stating it openly: "The ship *plows* the waves." When an identification is not put forth as an explicit proposition we are less likely to challenge it. . . . .

Judeo-Christian theology has consistently spoken and written of sex in metaphorical terms as a species of dirtiness. The identification of sexuality and dirtiness has been "built into" the psychological and neurological reactions of countless millions of people subliminally—without their being completely aware of the "poetic" or pre-logical nature of the identification.

When Romantic poets associate sexuality with budding flowers, growing grass, sprouting shrubs, and so on, they are creating an identification that points toward the opposite kind of reaction. Here we get the equation "sexuality equals spring-time" in contrast to the Judeo-Christian "sexuality equals dirtiness." Both equations are effective psychologically because they are poetic and imperfectly articulated.

"You see with your ears," the semanticist Count Alfred Korzybski used to say to his pupils. That is, unless we have made a specific effort to retain ourselves in *creative seeing,* as an artist does, we see what society (old verbal tapes in the back of our biocomputer) has *told* us to see. The words that you form in looking at a picture, in this book or anywhere, are words that have been *told* to you, sometime in the past. Who is seeing, then—you or the people who told you those words? *When* is the seeing—here and now, or back when those words were recorded on your computer tape? Dig: This is what the mystics mean when they say ordinary seeing is delusion; it's playing back old recordings. *Creative seeing,* real involvement with the world, is, like creative thinking, a volitional act.

The ostrich philosophy—what is not seen does not exist—is part of the way in which we lose contact with part of ourselves. "You have given away your eyes—other people have your eyes now," Frederick Perls used to say to students who hadn't learned *creative seeing*. He meant that just as the pathologically submissive person gives away his mind to others,[10] so, too, do most of us give away our vision. In the Catholic religion, priests and nuns figuratively give away their genitals; don't laugh at them until you're really sure you haven't given away something equally vital. William C. Shutz, Esalen psychologist, points out in *Here Comes Everybody* that any ordinary group of Americans, asked to move their conscious awareness through their bodies, upward from the toes to the crown of the head in stages—a quite ordinary yoga exercise—will encounter a variety of dead spaces; organs or parts in which there is no sensation at all. These are parts of themselves that have given away to society in return for social acceptability.

The surrender can be astonishingly total: Roman worshipers of Attis literally gave up their genitals by castrating themselves (there was a similar sect of Christians in Russia at one time). Some people wear dark glasses ("shades") even after sunset, constricting vision to the maximum degree possible. "I didn't hear you! I didn't hear you!" screams the producer in Norman Mailer's novel *The Deer Park* when told something he prefers to ignore. Hysterical malfunctions without organic damage are well recorded in psychiatric literature: hysterical blindness, paralysis, deafness, impotence, frigidity. . . . And it is against this background that we must understand the breast repression of the Jesus Freaks, the 1920s and the Dark Ages.

The exact reason (or reasons) for covering the breasts—or any other part of the body—is still obscure. Psychologists and anthropologists have dozens of theories about why people first put clothes on themselves (something no other animal has ever done) and it must be said that all of these reasons sound plausible—until one reads the criticisms of them by those savants who hold opposing theories. It is far from proven that we originally donned clothing to keep warm (the custom may well have originated in the tropics). Magic probably had a lot to do with the first garments—after all, you can't tell the priests from the audience without a costume, especially at the rowdy kind of religious observance our ancestors seem to have preferred. Modesty, so-called (the desire to hide certain sexual parts), may have provoked men and women to invent clothing—as Genesis suggests— but many theorists have argued quite plausibly that the clothing came first and the feelings of modesty later. To add to the complexity of the mystery, it is well documented that in many temples of the ancient Mediterranean cults, people *took clothes off* to show respect for the gods just as piously as a modern American girl may change from a miniskirt to something longer before entering a Protestant church. Taking clothes off for religion probably makes more sense than putting them on. It shows that one is approaching the divinity without any pretense or social role-playing, in a spirit of true humility.

Clothes are intimately related to cosmetics, tattoos and similar decorations. The case for nudism, as stated by its exponents, is entirely similar to Hamlet's objections to cosmetics in Shakespeare's tragedy: "God gave you one face and you make yourself another." God, the nudist says, gave me one body, and whenever I put on clothes I am disguising that and making myself a second, imitation body. Thus, the strict nudist objects to the renaissance custom of rouging the nipples to make them conspicuous as sternly (and with the same logic) as he objects to the modern custom of covering them with clothing. "Let us see the nipples God made," is his cry.

Clothes seem to have arrived on the scene around 75,000

to 100,000 years ago. The roots of modern intelligence, art, science, civilization, etc., seem to have been forming then also, along with the roots of modern neuroses, psychoses, wars, psychopathies, racial prejudices and other abominations. In short, clothing is a product of our ability to think *symbolically*. Other animals evidently can think only about what is right here, right now; but we can think about things that aren't here anymore or may be here in the future or may never be here. From this ability to abstract we produce our most glorious thoughts and out most frightful insanities. Whether clothing ranks as a glory or an insanity, of course, depends on your viewpoint; but wearing it is not something we would do if, like the dogs and apes and trees and fish, we only registered what is *right here, right now*.

It was the egregious Carlyle who first pointed out that clothing is almost entirely psychological in its functions. Writing of our primitive ancestor, the primordial hunter, Carlyle noted that "warmth he found in the toils of the chase; or amid dried leaves, in his hollow tree, in his bark shed, or natural grotto; but for decoration he must have clothes. The first spiritual want of a barbarous man is decoration. . . ." And of a barbarous woman.

Indeed, the kind of attention that women traditionally pay to other women's clothes is related to everything except their alleged use in protecting the body from bad weather. "Do you think my pearl necklace is too long?" a lady of lusty reputation once asked Madame de Pompadour. "Not at all," was the soft reply, "it is merely attempting to get back to its source." Zsa-Zsa Gabor could not have improved on that, except by adding a "Dahhhhling."

A maiden of the Upper Congo, where body paint, tattoo and scar patterns are used in precisely the same way, and for the same purpose, as the clothing of our own women, might seem well dressed when, actually, she is nude. The function is not to conceal or downgrade sexuality but to emphasize it in a new way. Lawrence Langner argues quite convincingly in his droll essay *The Importance of Wearing Clothes* that clothing is the chief cause of the year-round sexiness of human beings as compared to the only seasonal lasciviousness of other animals. It is quite true that nobody is as sexually stimulated in a nudist colony as he expects to be before he has tried a visit.

Of course, part of the sexually arousing effect of clothes resides in (a) the gradual revelation of nudity as they are slowly removed—the basis of that very interesting art form, the striptease; and (b) fantasies about removing them, as typified by men "undressing women with their eyes" on the street. ("There's a very sexy girl behind us," Holmes might have said to Watson on the street. "Gad, Holmes," the poor confused doctor would have cried "how can you see behind us?" "I can't; but I've been examining the expressions on the men coming toward us," would, of course, have been the answer.) Women's Liberation will never cure this male reflex unless the organization gets a law passed to castrate male infants shortly after birth.

The nude breasts of the Polynesians offended the missionaries, who forced the ladies to cover up with the well-known muu-muu or Mother Hubbard. The results, according to Arthur Grimble, research commissioner of Gilbert and Ellice Islands, were the opposite of those intended: "Clothes may have originated in the Garden of Eden but they have spoiled a Pacific paradise. Clothes covering bodies which once went naked have contributed to the natives' moral decadence by stimulating a nasty curiosity which never before existed." Charlie Chaplin made the same point with wonderful wit in an early short in which he is a house painter and comes upon a nude female statute in a room where he is painting. Charlie blushes, looks away, and then fetches a lamp shade which he places over the statute to cover the territory from breast to thighs. He then returns to his painting—for a few minutes, after which he creeps back and peeks under the shade lasciviously. That may be the whole psychology of clothing in a nutshell.

The same striptease or peakaboo effect underlies fashion, which keeps men interested from decade to decade by strategically changing which portion of the female anatomy will be revealed and which concealed. In a typical bit of 1920s cheesecake the withering away and down-playing of the breast is accompanied by a full display of legs, quite typical of that flat-chested and short-skirted decade. Similarly, when long skirts began to conceal legs in the late 1940s and early 1950s, designs were cut to emphasize buttocks—which also received great attention in the early pinups of PLAYBOY and its imitators. It is a general rule of female fashion: When something is being hidden, something else is being displayed. Thus, French women of the Napoleonic era quite boldly exposed their breasts in very low-cut gowns, but not an inch of leg showed: The shirt reached the floor. The striptease of fashion seem eternal: whatever is lost one decade returns the next, and whatever is gained is again lost.

It is worth pointing out that one item of clothing serves in itself to refute entirely all ideas that covering the body really attempts to achieve modesty. I refer, of course, to the brassiere—which has very little to do with making the breasts *less* conspicuous and everything to do with making them *more* conspicuous. The brassiere, in fact, has been designed and redesigned so often that it will do virtually anything, depending on the demands of the fashion of the moment. One bra will enlarge small breasts, another will conceal the size of large breasts; one will pull the breasts upward, another will flatten them downward; there is even an inflatable brassiere. Lawrence Langner's book on clothing quotes a joke about a bra manufacturer who produced three models: "The Great Dictator" (to suppress the masses), "The Salvation Army" (for uplift), and "The Yellow Press" (to make mountains out of molehills). In all of this, vanity, not modesty, is the true motive.

The braless look, once identified with Women's Libera-

tion although it actually preceded the political movement
by a few years in left-hippie circles, has to be understood as
a part of a context which includes such trends as: the no-
makeup look, the choice of cheap and "lower-class" clothing
(for both male and female), the resorting to yoga and chiropractics in place of traditional allopathic medicine, the choice
of hitchhiking as the preferred mode of travel, and possibly
even the choice of marijuana instead of alcohol as social drug.
In all this, the determining factor seems to be *a desire to avoid
spending money unnecessarily*; that is, to resist a system which
seems devoted chiefly to what the young call "ripping off"
the public. This is revolution in the anarchist form of direct
action, as contrasted with the political action urged by liberals and Marxists. It allows young people to quit jobs they
dislike, to travel extensively, to live on Welfare part-time,
to grab onto the freedom which the older generation has
mostly lost, just by accepting a certain amount of voluntary
poverty as the price of that freedom. The slogan, "Don't own
anything you can't pack in a knapsack and carry on your
back" is part of the same mystique, which is quite sane
actually, if one's motive in life is to enjoy oneself. It only
seems insane if one believes, like the older generation, that
the purpose of life is to impress the neighbors. (We will say
more about this new mentality, which Charles Reich has
called "Consciousness III," later on. There are ample reasons
to consider it just another passing fad. There are also reasons
to think it might be more than that and might represent an
irreversible change.)

The flat-breasted look of the 1920s is especially interesting since it paradoxically coincided with a great deal of
liberalism and general loosening of previous "Victorian" prudery. Sociologists emphasize the unisex or proto-women's-lib
aspect of what happened: Women were granted the vote in
1920 and surrended the typical female bust-line a few years
later; both were parts of a movement toward elimination of
sexual discriminations. But why then did feminism collapse

so thoroughly as the 1930s, 1940s and 1950s came and went—and why did it revive with such embittered and hysterical rhetoric in the late 1960s? For that matter, why did the flat breast coincide with the decline of breast-feeding for infants (a trauma which has left visible scars on the infants of that decade, who are now rather paranoid geriatric cases people quite hostile to all forms of life everywhere on the planet, including Blacks, Orientals, animals, Europeans, insets, fish and—most notable of all—their own children)? And why was the same decade the age of official repression of the most oral of all drug habits, alcohol, together with a total nationwide rebellion against the law never again equaled until the pot revolution of the 1960s? The psychodynamics of all this begs for clarification.

The Irish saying about a hard drinker, "He'd suck whiskey off a wounded leg," emphasizes the orality of the alcoholic. The simple-minded notion that alcoholism could be stopped by making all drinking illegal (similar to the anti-marijuana madness that began a decade later) coincides with the repression of orality of that epoch. There was not a single Democratic president in the decade of the 1920s and no "welfare" legislation that is remembered was passed by either House of Congress. When FDR ended alcohol prohibition and began distributing largesse to the one-third of the nation which he found "ill-fed, ill-clothed and ill-housed," the conservative H. L. Mencken found precisely the right metaphor for the change, saying Roosevelt was turning the government into "a milch-cow with 100,000,000 teats."

But meanwhile the "dry and lawless years" saw women's hair retreat to a vanishing point along with the female breast. The "boyish bob" hairstyle, like the long hair of the young males in the late 1960s, moved society toward a unisex look, with the change coming that time from the distaff side. Was this a denial of sexuality similar to that championed by some of the women's liberationists of the 1960s? Not quite—for the hem of the skirt began to rise, and rose again and again, and female legs are also sexual stimulants. The erotic signals driven away from the female form above the navel were replaced by a secondary concupiscence below the thighs. There seems to be a law of nature: Sex driven out the front door creeps back in through the side window.

Still: To any male born after 1930 (or even more, to any born after 1940) photographs of the "great beauties" of the 1920s are a strange and eerie sight. Women they certainly are; attractive women, indeed—BUT WHERE ARE THEIR BREASTS? Hidden beneath special brassieres which pulled them down and flattened them into a boyish look attractive only to latent homosexuals (who were officially not supposed to exist in that age of Republican rectitude, Harding-Coolidge-Hoover, old-fashioned gunboat diplomacy that lacked any unctuous pretense that the people we were invading had invited us, a seemingly ever-rising stock market, hip flasks and the naughty thrill of committing a crime every time you took a drink).

American women had surrendered their breasts, just as Wilhelm Reich in *Character Analysis*, Frederick Perls in *Gestalt Therapy Verbatim*, Alexander Lowen in *The Betrayal of the Body* and William C. Shutz in *Here Comes Everybody* describe patients who had given up parts of their bodies in order to evade the painful conflict between biological need and social hypocrisy. The repressed breast in the 1920s may be related to the hysterectomy fad of the 1930s, when doctors were finding dozens of reasons (now generally considered invalid) to remove the womb. In the 1940s, reporting on women who had mostly reached maturity in those decades, Kinsey found that two out of five of them were incapable of reaching orgasm until two years after beginning to have intercourse regularly. Perhaps all these symptoms were part of the price society had to pay in making the difficult transition from Victorian prudery to the contemporary "hang loose" ethic. In that case, a lot of the crazy behavior on all sides of us today can be comfortably accepted as evidence that we are still in transition toward some kind of sexual sanity.

Nevertheless, it must be granted that the repression of the breast, historically, has often indicated the presence of an anal mentality of a quite hostile nature. The nervous covering-up of the female bosom in the Dark Ages ushered in the epoch of witch-burning and mass hysterias. G. Rattray Taylor, in *Sex in History*, frankly categorizes the Europe of that period as "a cross between a madhouse and an abbatoir." The 1920s climaxed with 11,000,000 men unemployed and the government and corporations claiming alternately that they were unable to do anything about the situation or that the "lazy bums" *could so* find work if they'd only look harder. Aptly enough, the sex goddess of the decade was flat-chested Theda Bara (whose name, self-created, was an anagram on Death Arab, and who was widely billed as "The Vamp"—short for vampire).

Meanwhile, the first generation of infants was being raised without breast-feeding. A glass or plastic bottle with a rubber "nipple" was shoved at them to prevent physical death (what happened to the soul is anybody's guess, but, being now grown, these plastic-nursed individuals are called "plastic people" by rock singer-composer Frank Zappa. Similarly, a line from a popular 1960s movie, *The Graduate*— "Plastics, Benjamin, Plastics!"—applied to the same generation, immediately became part of folk speech, although few have traced this imagery back to its source in infant deprivation.) The female breast, in effect, had been banished from the United States, along with all legal booze. "Normalcy," an ungrammatical word at the time, but now accepted, was introduced by President Warren Gamiliel Harding ("Gamiliel the Stone-Head," in H. L. Mencken's estimation) and was the aim of the whole culture. "Normalcy" meant business-as-usual, everybody at his or her desk on time, a huge contempt of the "soft" (i.e., oral) ideas of radicals and the appearance in industry of "efficiency experts" dedicated to destroying the last vestiges of organic human rhythms and relationships on the assembly line to keep all "productive units," human and mechanical, moving to the ticking of one remorseless clock.

Yes, clocks—and preoccupation with time—are very anal, according to Freud. Father Time—the old man with the scythe who mowes us all down eventually—is a version of the punishing father god, his imagery directly derived from the Roman god Chronos (Time) who murdered his own children. The anal personality is created by rigid toilet-training schedules and remains preoccupied with scheduling thing *on time*.

There was even a fad, started in the 1920s, of "schedule-feeding" for infants. This teaching, which brought the anal temperament directly into the oral stage, insisted that infants should be fed at exactly the same times each day, no matter how hungry they became in the meantime, no matter how loud they screamed, no matter how instinctively guilty the mother felt listening to their terrified and enraged wails. The infants, lacking any sense of time or predictability, no doubt thought on each occasion (to the extent that they thought at all) that the food supply had been cut off permanently and they were about to starve. Eventually this sadistic doctrine— which was presented with great scientific "authority," like the masturbation terror which convinced Victorians that any boy who pulled on his wand would go crazy, and the antimarijuana crusade of more recent date—collapsed entirely when mothers simply rebelled against it. Psychiatrists and pediatricians today almost uniformly condemn it, yet it is not something (like female circumcision) performed by ignorant savages in backward areas; it was done in the 1920s and early 1930s right here. The infants it was done to are now our (understandably) jumpy and suspicious 50- and 60-year-old citizens. One novelist of that age, a very talented man, once told me that almost his entire psychoanalysis was concerned with unearthing the effects which this schedule-feeding had had on his psyche. He still doesn't like women much. A woman I know, who also went through this ordeal, tells me she only forgave her mother when she found, rummaging through the family library, that *all* the medical books they owned had recommended it as the most scientific and up-to-date theory. She now hates doctors and in raising her own children follows nothing but her own intuition and compassion.

Obviously, the flattening of the breast with special brassieres that pulled it down, the fad of the slim "boyish" look for women, the switching of infants from the breast to the bottle, the rise of "efficiency" and what Harry Truman was later to call "dinosaur conservativism" in industry, the decline of our native radical traditions like Populism, the triumph of puritanical and reactionary religiosity in such matters as the Prohibition Law and the banning of teaching evolution in schools, the sadistic tendency evidenced in schedule-feeding, the sudden rebirth of the Ku Klux Klan (which became more powerful in the 1920s than at any time since the 1870s), the witch-hunt atmosphere shown by the Palmer Raids (in which folk-singing societies were sometimes arrested *en masse* if the local patriots couldn't find any real socialists) as well as by the later-admitted frame-up of union organizer Tom Mooney and the probable frame-up of Sacco and Vanzetti—all indicate a strong swing toward what G. Rattray Taylor calls a "patrist" orientation and the Freudians call anality. The fact that this went along with, rather than against, an improvement of the status of women (in contrast to Taylor's patrist-matrist chart given later on page 88) should remind us that no period fits the generalizations of social scientists' "laws" exactly, and that if history repeats, it always repeats with differences. Nevertheless, the period largely fits Taylor's schema, as do large epochs of the Middle Ages, the Empire period in Rome, etc. F. Scott Fitzgerald's booze-drinking free-lovers were not representatives of that era but rebels against it, like the pot-smoking hippies of the 1960s.

The present author is not learned enough in sociology to attempt to say *what* caused *what*. The present tendency in the social sciences, however, is to abandon simple cause-effect and to describe clusters that seem to "hang" together, as I have just done. The questions, "did the flat-breast look cause the efficiency experts to appear? Did efficiency experts cause the flat-breast look? Did Prohibition cause the banning of the teaching of evolution?" etc., may just be versions of the old chicken-and-egg riddle. In any event, the present multanimity (a word coined by historian Crane Brinton to signify the opposite of unanimity) in the social sciences gives us no cause to expect answers until some major break-through places the whole field of human studies on a more scientific basis. In the meantime, we can at least note that the existence of these cultural clusters or configurations is becoming generally recognized, however much the interpre-tations may differ.

There is a story that Leo Frobenius, the German anthro-pologist who turned Pablo Picasso on to African art and Ezra Pound to African poetry, once looked at a certain pot and said, more or less, "If we go where that was found and dig, we will find traces of a culture having the following seven traits." He listed them; and after that, when an expedition was assembled and the digging was accomplished, Frobenius was proven right. This is not witchcraft or even ESP. Frobe-nius, the creator of the cluster concept—*kulturmophologie*, he called it—was acting on the principle that a tribe which creates a certain kind of pot will create a religion, an eco-nomic system, a fishing or hunting technique, a sexual ethic, etc., that all show the same preoccupations.

Thus, the reader who has been following the clusters we have presented here, on being told that the women in ancient Crete, off the perimeter of Greek culture, wore no coverings on their breasts and even forced them upward into a prominent position, should be able to make a few educated guesses about Cretan culture. In fact, the Cretans did have most of the oral qualities, including worship of a mother goddess, sexual freedom and high status for women. Similarly, the fact that naked breasts began to appear in European painting around 1415, after being banned for centuries, should lead one to make some guesses about events following 1415; and, in fact, this was a turning point in the decline of the papal-patriarchal control of Europe and the renaissance of oral and matrist values.

Of course, we are not asserting that the mere appearance of a nipple in public will bring all the other oral values in its wake; socially, causality is more complicated than that. (The Chinese saying, "When the music changes, the walls of the city shake," often quoted by writers on Rock, does not imply causality but what Jung calls synchronicity, as in the philosophy of the *I Ching*. The Chinese Taoist observes that changes in music and in politics occur together but does not attempt to convert one into the "cause" of the other; the notion that cause-and-effect explains all situations, or is applicable to all situations, is strictly an Occidental and Aristotelian invention.) Nevertheless, any item in a cluster can be taken as a sign or omen that the others must be on their way. The rooster's crow doesn't "cause" the dawn, but the dawn is certainly on its way when you hear him. When the breast withers away to a vanishing point, other oral and maternal values are also drying up and atrophying; when the breast sprouts forth again, these values are also returning.

By no accident, the most admired poem among American intellectuals in the 1920s was T. S. Eliot's *The Waste Land*; although actually dealing with his adopted country, England, his symbols spoke very eloquently to American sensibilities also. The withdrawal of the breast is suggested in Eliot's images of wandering in the desert, of thirst, of the failed crops in the land ruled by an impotent king, of sterility in general. The most famous of Eliot's images—e.g., "lilacs out of dead land," "The Hanged Man," "the Unreal City," "the corpse you planted last year in your garden," "rock and no water and the sandy road"—all revolve around the theme of life struggling to survive without nourishment. The final section, in the mountains (breast symbols, according to Freud), brings the promise of rain and renewal. If all poets seek to summon the mother goddess in her guise as Muse, Eliot in a very real sense is calling for her to appear as wet nurse. But before looking at how the 1930s began to answer that invocation, we should examine the historical background of mammary metaphysics a bit. That is the topic of our next chapter.

[9] *Psychology Today*, December 1972.

[10] Wilhelm Reich points out in *The Mass Psychology of Fascism* that—before it was necessary to flee Nazi Germany—he often argued with Nazi party members. When unable to explain or justify some action of Hitler's, they would inevitably resort to, "But he must have information you and I don't know about." One can hear the same remark from any submissive personality in America today if one forces him to confront a spectacularly irrational act by the god or fuhrer he happens to be following. Cf. Jesus's remark about the blind leading the blind.

4. Mammary Metaphysics

It has often been observed that there is a marked similarity between the words for *matter* in Indo-European languages (Latin *materium*, French *matière*, etc.) and the words for measurement (French *metre*, English *measure*, etc.). More interestingly, both groups seem to relate to the words for *mother* (Latin *mater*, German *mutter*, French *mère*). The earliest calendar, or device for measuring time, dated at around 30,000 B.C. has a distinctly female figure marking every 28th day. This figure has not yet been explained—a Cro-Magnon women's attempt to figure out her menstrual cycle? A schedule for the rituals of the moon goddess? In either event, it seems that the starry cosmos, in those days, was conceived as a great mother who had given birth to the life of the earth. Wise old women (the *wiccas*, wise ones, from whom we get the word *witches*) were thought to have a special affinity with her. Above all, this goddess was not a metaphor or an idea;

she was a living presence, just as the American Indians to this day refer to the earth as a living mother and still fondly expect that eventually she will throw off the maniacal whites whose technology seems to be largely an attack on her. Quite similarly, the early Romans conceived the thickest band of stars in the sky as the *Via Galactica*, the Way of Milk, from which we get our familiar expression the Milky Way. To them and to the Greeks this was literally a mist of milk across the heavens, spurted upward from the breasts of the earth-goddess, Hera.

Goethe's *Faust* provides a classic example of the same breast quest conveyed in a different symbolism:

FAUST:
A lovely dream once came to me;
I then beheld an apple tree,
And there two fairest apples shone;
They lured me so I climbed thereon.

YOUNG WITCH:
Apples have been desired by you
Since first in Paradise they grew;
And I am moved with joy to know
That such within my garden grow.

Freud commented tersely on this exchange: "There is not the slightest doubt what is meant by the apple-tree and the apples." In fact, *a nice apple-dumpling shop* is Cockney slang for a pair of firmly rounded breasts.

Some readers will be thinking of the Garden of Eden at this point, and they are probably right. It has long puzzled and provoked scholars that both Eve in that story, and the Goddess Eris in Greek mythology, are associated with *apples* and that the apples in both cases made a great deal of trouble. In the Hebrew story, Eve insists on eating a certain apple (actually, Genesis only says *fruit*, but tradition has always identified it with the apple), and Yehweh, the local volcano-god, is thrown into a fury and curses her and all mankind, for reasons that are far from perfectly clear. In the Greek story, Zeus slights Eris by not inviting her to a banquet on Olympus and she gets her revenge by manufacturing a golden apple inscribed KALLISTI ("To the prettiest one") and rolling it into the banquet hall. Immediately all the goddesses begin squabbling, each claiming to be the prettiest one and entitled to the apple; this quarrel worsens until men as well as gods are drawn into it and eventually the Trojan War results. Eris became known as the goddess of chaos and the golden apple is called the apple of discord.

The similarities here—the role of the female, the presence of the apple, the sequence of supernatural calamities— suggest that there might be a common origin to these myths. Such is indeed the case, according to Joseph Campbell's monumental four-volume study, *The Masks of God*. The Genesis text is very late and has altered the original myth to fit the patriarchal context of the religion of Yehweh. Originally, Eve was not Adam's wife, but his mother; she was not a human, but a goddess; and the outcome was not tragic, but triumphant—after the magic fruit was eaten, Adam himself became a god. (There is still a hint of this in the Genesis version, in which Yehweh says nervously, "Behold, the man has become as one of us [the gods], to know good and evil.") What was originally involved was probably a psychedelic sacrament, like the Eleusinian festival in Athens, in which the worshipers ate certain (hallucinogenic) foods and became one with the Mother Goddess Demeter. Eve and Eris, in short, are negative patriarchal versions of the *bona dea* (good goddess) of Rome, the earthmother whose milk covers the sky at night, the Isis of Egypt, Ishtar of Babylon, the all-protective figure who has descended directly from the huge-breasted Venus of Willendorf—that numinous deity who is just an extension on the cosmic scale of the vision of the infant at the breast.

Nor is she entirely dead yet. Robert Graves in *The White*

Goddess insists that all true poets have a vision of her at some time or other, at the very least in their dreams. Contemporary witch covens still worship her and I have personally attended a quite beautiful ceremony—in Minneapolis, Minnesota, no less—in which she was invoked and spoke through the watch queen to declare:

> You shall be free, and as a sign that you be really so, be naked in your rites, dance, sing, feast, make music and love. All in my praise, for I am a gracious goddess, who gives joy upon earth; certainty, not faith, while in life; and upon death peace unutterable, rest and the ecstasy of the goddess. Nor do I demand aught in sacrifice, for behold, I am the mother of all living, and my love is poured out upon the earth.

This is quite lovely, I think; and it is also, beyond debate, a purely oral religion. The goddess is an extension of the infant's picture of the breast, if the breast could speak. Thus, Wolfgang Lederer, M.D., describes the great mother goddess as virtually an extension in space-time of the breasts themselves:

> Her breasts, for instance, for the sake of which the Babylonians called her "The Mother with the fruitful breasts," she whose breasts never failed, never went dry . . . they were occasionally . . . reduced to stylized rings or spirals, but they were more often lustily stressed, and most impressively so by multiplication. The great Diana of Ephesus is usually represented with numerous breasts—I count up to 16—and the Mexican Goddess of the Agave, Mayauel, has 400. Their function is obvious enough, and some of the most beautiful and touching icons of the goddess show her with the infant at her breast, whether she be the Egyptian Isis with the child Horus or her equivalent in Asia Minor, Ur, prehistoric Sardinia, Mexico and Peru or contemporary Africa, or of course one of the innumerable virgins with child of Christian art: these, especially during the later middle ages, accomplish such tenderness and intimacy of expression, such union of animal warmth and purest

spirituality, that one is easily long lost in contemplation. . . .

Moreover, the Goddess we describe is no mere human mother, giving human milk to the child of her flesh and blood, nor yet simply a divine mother, with a child human or divine: for from her nipples may flow, not milk, but honey—as in Palestine, which was the land of milk and honey on her behalf, or at Delphi, where her priestesses were called *Melissai*—"bees"— and her shrine was likened to a beehive. Or, wonderful to behold, all kinds of fishes may drop from her nipples, as among the Eskimo. Indeed, she not only gives birth to all manner of animals, she also feeds them, giving each what it needs, and "Alma Mater" that she is, she may—wonder of wonders—give such to bearded men, to scholars, feeding them wisdom. She is, in short, the source of all food, material or spiritual.

No wonder she is proud of her breasts. And, hence, quite naturally, she holds them, either to show them off, or to offer more conveniently their fullness . . .[12]

Statues of the goddess, holding her breasts in this "offering" position, have been found all over prehistoric Europe and Asia. They must have been, at one time, as common as the more familiar mother-with-child later adopted by Roman Christianity.

In contrast, and despite the orality of Jesus himself, the Judeo-Christian faiths are strongly anal[13] and their stern Father God demands endless sacrifices, offers no joy on earth but only duty blindly obeyed, and threatens sadistic tortures (for an infinite numbers of years, according to some theologians) to anyone who crosses him. It almost seems as if history, at least in the Occident, repeats the pattern Freud found in the nursery, from oral bliss to anal anxiety.

This was the opinion, in the last century, of the German folklorist J. Bachofen, of the American anthropologist Lewis Morgan, and of Karl Marx's financial supporter and collaborator, Freidrich Engels. Their hypothesis of a single historical pattern, in which all societies evolve from matriarchal communism to patriarchal capitalism (and then back to communism, according to Engels), was widely accepted for about 50 years, but then evidence that conflicted with it began accumulating. Some societies were never matriarchal; some alleged matriarchies were actually only matrilineal—that is, descent and property were passed through the female line, but men still held the chieftainships or governorships; and, if some of Bachofen's inspired guesses about prehistorical Europe were startlingly right, others were glaringly wrong. The theory of primordial matriarchy was rejected by anthropologists as thoroughly as the luminiferous ether was rejected by physicists. Only in the last few years has it had some revival, under the impact of new data collected and polemically proclaimed by female scholars more or less allied with the Women's Liberation Movement.

Meanwhile, Leo Frobenius in Germany, G. Rattray Taylor in England and Joseph Campbell in our country have all collected and published voluminous data showing that if the primitive matriarchy did not exist as universally as the 19th-Century theorists imagined, something much like it existed just before the dawn of recorded history in the West and Near East and coexisted with the first patriarchal civilizations for a while. The oral and gentle mother goddesses are a survival of that period, and there have been various attempts to revive its values in historical times. G. Rattray Taylor even provides a table[14] showing the differences between the two kinds of cultures, which he calls patrist and matrist. In strict Freudian terms they are, of course, respectively, anal and oral: (See chart page 79)

The much-debated thesis of Charles Reich in *The Greening of America* held that our country is passing from what he called Consciousness II to Consciousness III. It is obvious that Consciousness II is largely patrist (and anal), while Consciousness III is largely matrist (and oral). It is not surprising to a Freudian, then, that there was a progression from the fad of big-breasted movie stars in the 1940s (the thin edge of the matrist wedge) to the breakthrough of

Patrist (anal)	Matrist (oral)
1. Restrictive attitude toward sex	1. Permissive attitude toward sex
2. Limitation of freedom for women	2. Freedom for women
3. Women seen as inferior, sinful	3. Women accorded high status
4. Chastity more valued than welfare	4. Welfare more valued than chastity
5. Politically authoritarian	5. Politically democratic
6. Conservative: against innovation	6. Progressive: revolutionary
7. Distrust of research, inquiry	7. No distrust of research
8. Inhibition, fear of spontaneity	8. Spontaneity: exhibition
9. Deep fear of homosexuality	9. Deep fear of incest
10. Sex differences maximized (dress)	10. Sex differences minimized (dress)
11. Asceticism, fear of pleasure	11. Hedonism, pleasure welcomed
12. Father-religion	12. Mother-religion

PLAYBOY's barebreasted pinups in the 1950s and 1960s, to hippiedom and women's lib in the 1960s and 1970s. It is also quite natural that each new wave has regarded the previous wave as a sick and compromised part of the old patrist regime.

It is curious, in passing, that the Women's Liberation Movement, the latest and most revolutionary of these waves, is paradoxically more patrist than much of what preceded it chronologically. It is unfortunate that some women operating under the banner of "women's liberation" have simply adopted the worst characteristics of patriachical men and then declared the result to be "freedom." This is noteworthy in regard to Taylor's points 1, 4, 5, 7, 8 and 11—permissiveness versus restriction, welfare versus chastity, authoritarianism versus democracy, attitude toward research, inhibition versus spontaneity and ascetism versus hedonism. On all of these issues the liberationists are distinctly moving backward toward an anal-patrist orientation rather than forward toward oral-matrist "Consciousness III." They not only incline toward Victorian prudery, but have revived the old Victorian delight in sexual slander and blackmail. Just as the great Irish rebel, Charles Steward Parnell, fell into disgrace and was ruined when his adultery with Kitty O'Shea was discovered and denounced by the Catholic clergy, many radical heroes have been cast down from their previous eminence when these ladies published sexual exposés of them (with names omitted, but all other details immediately recognizable) in their magazines. (Sometimes the names are included, as recently happened to a gentle Black pacifist, who was not even accused of unethical acts but just of having the wrong ideas, but who nonetheless suffered the humiliation of having his mind, soul, body and his "golden penis," no less, roundly condemned in several issues of a radical journal.) Not only are their dogmas sacrosanct, democratic discussion scorned and scientific research rejected (as "male"), but many of them have announced that reason itself is deeply suspect and now frankly embrace the "credo quia absurdum" ("I believe because it is absurd") of the church fathers.

Rejection of science and of free discussion are, of course, characteristic of all totalitarian movements; thus, nonbiblical astronomy was heretical to the Inquisition, unpalatable anthropology was "Jewish" to the Nazis, unsatisfactory biology was banned as "bourgeois" in Stalin's Russia and irritating ethology is "sexist" (and unpleasant psychology is "chauvinist") to these ladies. Like all other totalitarian fiats, this is intellectually protected by concentric circles of similar rhetoric. Thus, to question the concept of witchcraft or heresy in the days of the Inquisition automatically meant that one was a witch or a heretic. To say that science is neither Jewish nor gentile, socialist nor bourgeois, but merely the activity of independent minds attempting to be objective, opened one to suspicion of being "Jewish" in Germany or "bourgeois" in Russia. To say that behavioral sciences cannot be dismissed with epithets like "sexist" and "chauvinist" is to convince these ladies that the speaker is "sexist" and "chauvinist." To push the argument one step further and say that such protective rationalization prevents objective inquiry is to encounter the same rhetoric in a third concentric armor and again to be charged with heresy, Jewishness, bourgeois tendencies or sexism, etc. At the furthest extreme, where communication has been reduced to the mere stubborn hope of trying to communicate, is the *"credo quia absurdum"* or, in its modern form, "You're just being rational—can't you *feel* the truth?" At this point reason retires from the field, defeated as usual by the will to believe.

One is reminded of a story about Mark Twain and his very fashionable and respectable New England wife, who once tried to cure him of his salty riverboat speech. Mrs. Twain noted every cuss word he used all week long and then woke him Sunday morning and read it all back to him. Twain listened calmly and commented, "You have the words, my dear, but you haven't got the music yet."

Women's liberationists have the words of freedom, equality, human dignity, etc., but they haven't got the music at all. Perhaps this is due to the strongly anal and Germanic influence exerted by Karl Marx. But a young friend of mine, more ingeniously, explains it as the desiderata of the large number of ex-nuns in the women's lib camp who have brought with them the pontifical attitudes of the Roman patriarchy. Nonetheless, the movement is the latest wave of an obvious matrist floodtide and as such destined to play a large role in the next few decades. Let us hope that its shell of dogma will be softened by the noisy splashing of all the other odd and colorful fish swimming about in the free waters of Consciousness III.

Meanwhile, the many books proving that everything

worthwhile was invented by women (like the equally excellent tomes by Black liberationists proving that all culture is of Negro origin) at least have the virtue of reminding us of the bias that makes most history texts sound as if all progress is owing to White males. It is now fairly evident that the earliest civilizations around the fertile crescent including the Nile and Euphrates were quite matrist in orientation; some may have been, as Bachofen thought, actually matriarchal, or very close to it. In Babylon, Minoan Crete, early Egypt and Etruscan Italy it appears that the chief deity was the great mother, whose statues, showing her with bared breasts, look remarkably alike whether her local name be Astarte, Ishtar, Isis or Ashtoreth. Women served as judges, priestesses, and, it appears, sometimes as governors. They had all the rights of men, could buy and sell property, engage in business, sign contracts, obtain easy divorce and they were widely considered to have a capacity superior to males in understanding what the goddess wanted and expected of her human children. From all one can gather, they had none of the misanthropy of current women's lib types or of the 19th-Century suffragettes. But why should they have hated men? At that stage, men had apparently never oppressed them.

"History begins with the emergence of men from female rule," Robert Graves has written, with slight exaggeration, in *Mammon and the Black Goddess*. Other historians, without any obvious promale or antifemale bias, still dissent from this broad view and suggest that female rule (in the manner of the male rule we are familiar with in later times) was comparatively rare and that something more like that elusive ideal *sexual equality* seemed to prevail in these early city-states. More remarkable yet, the absence of defenses or other signs of embattlement around these sites has convinced many archaeologists that there was no organized warfare, either, and it even seems that slavery itself did not emerge until much later. Will Durant, in *The Story of Civilization*, quoting a wide sampling of the best archaeological evidence, argues persuasively that slavery was created *after* the subjugation of women *and was probably inspired by it*.

In China, curiously, a very similar pattern has been discerned by contemporary scholarship. As Joseph Needham demonstrates in a remarkable six-volume study, *Science and Civilization in China*, the matrist and matriarchal values there were preserved in that remarkable text, the *Tao Tê Ching*, which praises a figure quite cognate with the great goddess of the Mediterranean area:

The Valley Spirit never dies
She is called the Eternal Woman

and urges all the usual matrist qualities already listed in the table from G. Rattray Taylor. Needham concludes that Chinese culture, before the Chou dynasty, was probably matrilineal and vaguely along the lines of Bachofen's classic matriarchies.

Even after the rise of the patriarchal governing class, women retained most of their traditional rights in Sparta until well within historical times. (Plato, whose *Republic* is considered pro-Spartan propaganda by some historians, included equality for women in his ideal nation, along with such other Spartan institutions as state socialism and lamentable Stalinist censorship of the arts.) Even in Athens, where the wives were reduced to a condition only slightly above that of the slaves, the courtesan class had most of the freedom enjoyed by nonslave males. The Athenians seem to have made the great divorce between sexual love and sexual reproduction that characterizes so many later societies. Their lyric poems are almost always written to courtesans or to young boys; they never seem to have felt romantic about the women who mothered their children.

Throughout these first pagan patriarchies, however, love and sex were still enjoyed and praised as great ornaments of life and inextricably connected with the religious life. The

Old Testament, like the popular marriage manuals circa 1920–1960, glorifies sex in marriage as the highest of human joys—and does not neglect the breasts. ("Rejoice with the wife of thy youth . . . Let her breasts satisfy thee at all times," Proverbs 5:18–19.) The Song of Solomon even seems, to the literalminded reader, to be praising fornication—but subtle rabbis and Christian theologians have repeatedly argued that it means quite the opposite of what it appears to say. (Actually, as Robert Graves has noted, the Song looks very much like the chants which accompanied rites of fertility-magic in the old matriarchal religion or in the still-surviving witch cult.)

Early Egyptian religion, it might be noted, was largely sexual in basis and totally concerned with the great mother goddess, variously known as Nuit, Isis, Nu-Isis, etc. Set, the snake god, representing the phallus, was the only male god in those days to achieve a rank roughly equal to the goddess, and only because he was necessary to her divine function as mother of all. (The phallic snake god, which the Egyptians acquired from the Congo region, still survives as an important figure in African and Haitian voodoo. Some cults derived therefrom survive in New Orleans and other parts of the American South.) The Nuit-Isis cults summarized their teaching in the aphorism, revived in our time by Aleister Crowley, "The Khabs is in the Khu." (*Khabs* is the divine or eternal part of humanity; *Khu* is the female genital, origin of our word *cunt*.) It is not "licentiousness" or lack of religion, but the *sexual* basis of their religion, that led the Egyptians to portray their gods in manners shocking to Christian observers: Atem depicted as masturbating, Isis as performing fellatio on her brother-husband Osiris, etc. Another biological depiction of Egyptian origin, Isis nursing the infant Horus, was however, acceptable to the Christians and some of these statues later found their way into Christian temples, with Isis renamed Mary and Horus changed to Jesus. But by then the meaning had been lost and, as Kenneth Grant

says in *The Revival of Magic*, the *physical* basis of Egyptian
religion had become the *metaphysics* of the Christian and
Hellenistic philosophers. That is, insofar as sex was admitted
into religion at all, *a la* the Song of Solomon, it was interpreted as a symbol of a spiritual relationship.

Homer's favorite adjective for well-stacked females was
bathykolpos, which means having ample breasts. Considering
that the poet was, according to all ancient sources, blind,
he must have learned to appreciate this feature by the braille
system, and he evidently enjoyed the experience. Interestingly enough, Homer's values are largely matrist. Some
have even suggested that Homeric works are older than
usually assumed and actually trace back to a quasi or totally
matriarchal period; Samuel Butler, Robert Graves and Eliza-
beth Gould have argued that "Homer" *was* a woman. Certainly, Homer regarded Achilles and the other military heroes in his poems as somewhat crazy and saved his real
affection for Odysseus, who started out as a draft-dodger,
went to the war reluctantly and always exercised his celebrated craftiness in trying to find a way to get home to his
beloved wife and away from all that pointless bloodshed. It
has also been observed that Homer has a special fondness
for the old goddesses and tends to treat Zeus as something
of a comic character, much like the old crank of later farcical
writers. Nevertheless, one modern women's lib writer, Nancy
R. McWilliams, has denounced Homer as male chauvinist
because Odysseus had all the fun of the Trojan War to
himself and didn't invite Penelope to come along and share
the butchery.

Whether Homer was a feminist, a male chauvinist or a
woman himself (herself?), he (she?) has all the qualities
found in recent male poets, who are notoriously antigovern-
ment, antiwar, antiauthority and fond of women, children,
nature and sexuality. Obviously, he was in Freudian terms
an oral personality. In any case, his values (and those of later
poets like Euripides, Sophocles, the anonymous authors of

the *Greek Anthology*, etc.) were compatible with sexual love, however much the relationship between men and women had been rendered problematical by the patriarchal system, which had reduced women to second-class citizens.

With the coming of Christianity, that last vestige of the old matrist system crumbled. Women became less than second-class citizens: They became outcasts, pariahs, tools of Satan to be feared and distrusted. Their breasts became, not a proof that the high gods loved the world and deliberately graced it with beauty, but a sly trap designed by Satan to lure men into fleshly sin. Women were "sacks of dung," according to Origen; they deserved to be treated like untrustworthy slaves, Augustine reasoned, because it was a woman, Eve, who had brought evil into the world; they were inclined to fornicate with devils, according to Sprenger the Inquisitor, because their lusts were too extreme to be satisfied by mortal men. If they were not all witches, the Fathers agreed solemnly, they certainly needed a lot of careful watching.

Considering that the current women's lib writers largely share the antisexual bias of the church fathers, it is curious that they haven't yet revived Augustine's celebrated argument that sexual *feeling* itself is a curse imposed upon as punishment for the sin of Adam and Eve. According to the bishop's curious reasoning, Adam and Eve, before the Fall, had no sexual feelings at all, and this is the way God intended us to be. To the question, "How did they manage to reproduce without sensation?" Augustine gave an answer that is worthy of the consideration of ladies like Ti-Grace Atkinson: The organs of generation, he says, moved by "Will Power." His defense of this assertion, probably the most influential flight of reasoning in the whole history of Christian theology, is worth reproducing:

> There are persons who can move their ears, either one at a time, or both together. There are some who, without moving the head, can bring the hair down upon their forehead, and move the whole scalp backwards and forwards at pleasure.

Some, by lightly pressing their stomach, bring up an incredible quantity and variety of things they have swallowed, and produce whatever they please, quite whole, as if out of a bag. Some so accurately mimic the voices of birds and beasts and other men that, unless they are seen, the differences cannot be told. Some have such command of their bowels that they can break wind continuously at pleasure, so as to produce the effect of singing.[15]

All such powers, Augustine claims, are remnants of the capacity of Adam's will to control his entire body; it was with such a mind-over-matter attitude that he and Eve approached sex, and not by the matter-over-mind compulsion that now acts upon us. This charming picture of the sexual, and other, acrobatics in the Garden of Eden was literally believed and any trace of the oral "oceanic feeling" (or any other kind of feeling) in the sex act was a sure sign of sin. Women, who provoked such streamings of energy in males by merely walking on the street, were obviously an extremely dangerous lot and the church took good care to see that any remaining rights they still possessed were quickly and thoroughly removed. In Catholic teaching, a woman was not allowed to divorce a man for beating her regularly, for catching V.D. and transmitting it to her, for bringing his girlfriends to the house and copulating before her eyes, for murder, for insanity, for torturing dogs in front of their children, or for any similar peccadillos. However, if he refused to produce new Catholics in her womb, and did not inform her before they were married that he had no intention of ever having children she could obtain an annulment of the marriage. (Recently the church liberalized grounds for annulment but only after the Italian government passed its first civil-divorce law over strenuous church opposition.)

To climax the degradation of women, the church has also ruled that in any difficult obstetric situation, where a choice between the life of the mother and the life of the child seems necessary, the doctor must strive to save the unborn.

At one time, this teaching extended to those abnormal preg-
nancies in which the fetus attached to the tube and could
not possible be born alive; even here, the doctor was supposed to try to save it, although it was known that this
would cost the life of the mother. (This ruling was only
changed in the 1930s.)

In all this, of course, we see Freud's famous "anal
personality" carried to its logical extreme. Although oral
persons tend to be more "reasonable" in the venacular sense
of that word, being more flexible and sympathetic to the
needs of others, anal persons worship reason and follow it
with remorseless tenacity wherever it leads, although often
having an equal capacity to ignore facts, which are after all
on the sensory or sensuous level and therefore somewhat
suspect. Augustine "proved" that unbaptized infants are unfit
for heaven; and, since purgatory and limbo hadn't been
invented yet, there was only one place left for them, hell.
This is shocking to modern sensibilities, but logic had led
Augustine to it and he was not a man to back down from a
logical position just because it seemed revolting to normal
human feelings. (Feelings, after all, were quite suspect: Adam
and Eve didn't have any, remember?) Less appalling, but
more amusing, Aquinas reasoned that female vultures are
fertilized by the wind, not by male vultures. A little observation, of the sort any empiricist would have undertaken before
publishing on the subject of vultures, could have prevented
such a blunder; but the Fathers were interested in logic,
pure logic, and facts were notoriously as illogical as feelings.

Of course, all this was a big pretense. Mr. Murdstone
told David Copperfield's mother that her loving kindness
was less "rational" than his sadism, and perhaps even believed it himself, but any psychologist will realize that Murdstone happened to enjoy caning little boys on the buttocks,
just as many Englishmen (for reasons peculiar to that culture)
still do. So, too, it is hard to escape the conclusion that the
church fathers enjoyed bullying, torturing and especially

frightening others, just as the members of the Gestapo did. De Sade in his marvelously frank way analyzed the joy in frightening people as a refined form of the sadist/ compulsions that drove him, and many psychoanalysts have noted the same connection. Sermons on hell, to hysterical and fainting congregations, are the psychological equivalent of the racks, whips, iron boots and other overtly sadistic implements of the Holy Inquisition.

The exact number of people killed in the various witch-hunts, crusades, inquisitions, religious wars, etc., is not recorded anywhere, but the total must run into the tens of millions; Homer Smith, an atheist, arrives at a figure of 60,000,000 in his *Man and His Gods*, but he is exaggerating (I hope). One Roman pagan skeptically remarked in the 4th Century A.D., that "there is no wild beast more blood-thirsty than an angry theologian." He had only seen the beginning of the feuds between various sects of Christians; the fury rolled on for another 13 centuries before it began to abate. Of course, Homer Smith's estimate of 60,000,000 victims is obtained by including all the Moslems killed in the several Crusades, and the non-Whites in Africa, the Americans and Oceana wiped out in the process of Christianizing the world. For Europe itself the very careful G. Rattray Taylor arrives at conclusions that make Hitler seem like a piker compared to the churchmen:

> In Spain, Torquemade personally sent 10,220 persons to the stake. . . . Counting those killed for other heresies, the persecutions were responsible for reducing the population of Spain from twenty million to six million in two hundred years. . . . While the well-known estimate of the total death-toll, from Roman times onward, of nine million is probably somewhat too high, it can safely be said that more persons were put to death than were killed in all the European wars fought up to 1914.[16]

Let us all piously hope that the current mood of tolerance

among Christian clergymen is not just a passing fad but that it represents a real break with their tradition. Still with the resurgence of the so-called Fundamentalist Christians, (i.e., Christian groups committed to the *necessity* of Armageddon to fulfill their theological dogma) we may yet see Christianity in its classic bloddy fury on the march again.

The whole story of the Christian blood-lust is the most distressing tale in history, especially when one remembers that it was all started by a gentle Jewish philosopher who preached love and forgiveness. For our purposes here, the saga of Christian rage illustrates what happens when the repression of the breast and of all oral values is carried to an extreme, and when humorless men reason logically from supernatural and unproven premises to their inevitable conclusions. It was permissible to torture the accused during the witch-hunt mania because in no other way could confessions be obtained in great numbers, and everybody knew that there *must be* great numbers of witches. It was permissible to promise mercy in order to get a confession and then to break the promise by burning the accused at the stake—this was technically no lie because it was truer than ordinary truth. They were being saved from hell, and so they did obtain mercy after all. The earth was the center of the universe because the Bible says so—if telescopes led to different conclusions, they were instruments of the devil. Children of witches should be compelled to watch their mothers burn at the stake—this was the only way to undo the wrong teachings they must have acquired from her.

Does all this sound absurd and hideous to you? In Freudian terms, that is because a great many oral and female values have crept back into our society in the last few centuries. None of this sounded absurd or hideous to the totally anal personalities of men like Augustine and Aquinas and Luther. They were not mad, but coldly logical: They never believed anything that they could not prove in neat, technically precise syllogisms. In the last century, the great mathematician George Boole even proved that the whole methodology of theological logic could be converted into mathematical equations, and every bit of it was sound, internally consistent and valid—once the original assumptions were granted. There was nothing wrong with the brains of the theologians. It was simply that their feelings had atrophied. Later, when we examine Jungian psychology and the Hindu *chakras*, we will see that banishing the goddess archetype had impoverished their sensibility and deadened certain emotional centers which we now assume are innate in all human beings. They are not; all emotions must be exercised and nourished, just like muscles, or they atrophy. The church fathers had entirely disposed of all oral components. **The fact that the female breast was banished from European art for several centuries means much more than appears at first glance.** That denial of one part of the human body did not "cause" all the other strange behaviors we have chronicled, but it was certainly related to them. When the breast began to stage a comeback, oral values in general began to reappear in European culture.

The first early waves of the new paganism appeared in southern France in the 11th and 12th centuries. Ideas from the Sufis and other Arabian mystics began to find an audience. The sexual doctrines of the Sufis, involving semiritualized intercourse with a beloved female as a specifically religious act, found a particularly enthusiastic support in certain circles—and have gone on to influence the vocabulary of our poets ever since, as Ezra Pound first demonstrated in his *Spirit of Romance* and as Denis de Rougemont has shown at even greater length in *Love in the Western World*.

Overtly, the new spirit began with Eleanor of Aquitaine, whose reputed bare-breasted ride through Jerusalem may or may not have actually happened, but has been widely believed for centuries. This was in many ways a historical turning point, and obviously much more was involved than a mere prank. At the very least, Eleanor showed a great sense of appropriate symbolism. Like freckle-faced Phyrne, Eleanor seems to have cherished both her beauty and her intellect and could not be persuaded by any male priesthood of a male god that she should hide either. (There were no Marxian feminists around to tell her she was making herself a "sex object.") She also seems to have convinced a large segment of the French nobility that love is a greater sport than war and that a man who wrote love poems was more virile than a conqueror of cities. This led to the outbreak of Provençal "troubadour" poetry and the similar verse of the minnessingers in South Germany, along with the famous "Courts of Love" in which subtle points of sexual etiquette and romantic decorum were taught. The cynical remark that "love was invented in the 12th Century" is not true, but it is emphatically true that most of our modern ideas about love were invented then, largely due to Eleanor's influence. A song about her—

> I would give the whole world
> From the Red Sea to the Rhine
> If the Queen of England tonight
> In my bed were mine

—has survived eight centuries and was recently set to modern music by Carl Orff as part of his popular "Carmina Burana" suite. Actually, after becoming Queen of England Eleanor had a rather bad time. Her husband, Henry II, a jealous type, put her under house arrest in a rather lonely castle and interrupted her personal involvement with the cultural revolution she had instigated.

The revolution, however, continued. The troubadour cult of love became a powerful rival to the church's cult of asceticism and the feudal lords' cult of war; the role of women was steadily elevated—and, as Ernest Jones pointed out in his psychoanalytical history of chess, the role of the queen on the chessboard changed from the weakest to the strongest piece. Strange and radical doctrines were preached by groups like the Cathari, who seem to have practiced the same kind of sexual occultism that Aleister Crowley revived in our own century; the Beguines, independent women who established their own religious order outside the Catholic hierarchy; the Knights Templar, who combined Christianity with Sufi sex-mysticism learned in Jerusalem; and the Brethren of the Common Purse, who practiced voluntary communism. Eventually, the church itself was infected with the new spirit, and the Mother of Jesus, a shadowy and insignificant figure previously, advanced, like the queen in chess, to a dominant position which she still holds in orthodox Catholic countries. As a sort of climax, the greatest of all Catholic poets, Dante, made his childhood sweetheart, Beatrice Portinari, so important in his *Divine Comedy* that she inadvertently overshadows Jesus, God the Father and even the Virgin Mary herself, making this orthodox Christian poem a more exalted personal love-lyric than the deliberately heretical poems in which the French troubadours had blasphemously raised their mistresses and girl friends above the saints. Pierre Vidal was knowingly and flagrantly toying with Sufi heresy when he wrote, "I think I see God when I look upon my lady nude," but Dante got the same effect without realizing quite what he was doing.

Vidal, in fact, can be considered in some ways the model of the new love-oriented man that Eleanor had set up as a contrasting ideal to the warrior or the saint. Half-mad or totally mad, Vidal was nonetheless a master craftsman of rhyme whose verse is still praised for its technical perfection and exuberance. The victim or hero of his own infatuations and the constant scrapes they landed him in, he even on one occasion convinced a whole town that he was a werewolf in order to impress a lady who had turned him down. He not only convinced her and the town, but did such a good job that a panic started and he had to flee. He was hunted with dogs through the hills around Arles (where Van Gogh also went mad and saw cosmic visions seven centuries later—

locals attribute such brain fevers to the *mistral* or "that damned
wind" as they call it). Vidal finally was brought to trail for
witchcraft and barely escaped being burned at the stake.
Times change. Now (1989) with the witch hunt revival and
Reefer Madness, million of people are being told they must
participate in the New Inquisition of pissing into a bottle
while someone watches. Then they are graded on the chemical analysis of their urine.

Somewhat similar, although less bizarre, was the case
of Sordello (hero of a very inaccurate poem by Browning),
who persuaded a married lady, Cunniza da Romano, to
elope with him. In a Europe still totally Catholic, there was
no way of legalizing such a relationship, but Sordello and
Cunniza evidently trusted the heretical "Courts of Love"
more than the dusty tomes of the church fathers. (Dante,
curiously, did not put either of them in his Hell. Sordello is
in Puragatory, and, odder yet, Cunniza is in Paradise—
because she freed her slaves. A number of scholars have
questioned Dante's orthodoxy.) For Cunniza, Sordello wrote
what Ezra Pound among others has praised as the noblest
hyperbole in the history of love poetry:

> If I see you not, lady with whom I am entranced,
> No sight I see is worth the beauty of my thought.

This kind of thing evidently become commonplace: The
troubadour Cabestan was murdered by a jealous husband
who then (possibly considering himself a figure in Greek
tragedy) cut out poor Cabestan's heart and served it at
dinner to his faithless wife, telling her it was a deer's. When
she had enjoyed it, the scoundrel told her what it had
actually been, and she threw herself from a balcony and died
on the rocks below. This near-incredible but true story is
dramatized in Pound's *Canto 4* and Richard Aldington's
"The Eaten Heart"; I cannot imagine why Puccini did not
make an opera of it.

Eventually, the Knights Templar were suppressed by

the Inquisition (123 of them were burned at the stake after being tortured into confessing a long string of abominations which most historians regard as fictitious) and the Albigensian Crusade was launched—ostensibly against the sexually permissive Cathari sect—but once rolling, it decimated the population of southern France in what Kenneth Rexroth has bitterly called "the worst atrocity in history, before the invention of Progress." The Templars did not revive until the 18th Century and the Cathari only came back in the 1920s. The papist patriarchy reconquered all Europe until the Protestant schism and retains Southern Europe to this day.

Romantic poetry with its matrist and oral values survived and actually prevailed. Geoffrey Chaucer imported the ideology to England with his *Knight's Tale* and some of his shorter rondels; by Elizabethan times this had virtually become the *whole* of poetry. Thus, Shakespeare could write about anything that struck his imagination when he was writing for the stage, but as soon as he started writing poetry for the printed page, he fell inevitably into the language, the themes, the traditional conceits and the entire apparatus of troubadour love-mysticism. So great was Shakespeare's influence, in turn, that when modern poets finally began writing about other subjects around 1910, established opinion was shocked and it was said that such material was "unpoetic"—as if Homer's battles, Ovid's mysticism, Juvenal's indignation, Villon's earthiness, Lucretius's rationalism, the *Greek Anthology's* cynicism, Piers Plowman's social protest, etc., had never existed and *only* the troubadour love-mystique had ever been poetry.

Considering how anal our culture had largely been, except for the matrist interlude of Eleanor and her circle, it is astonishing to realize that (just like our religious progenitor, Jesus) our most influential poet-dramatist, Shakespeare, was a distinctly oral type. A fairly consistent imagery of interrelated themes of sucking and chewing runs through all the plays and sonnets and has helped scholars determine

that contrary to more romantic theories they are all the work
of one person. (Examples: "Sucking the honey of his vows"
—*Hamlet*; "If music be the food of love, play on" —*Twelfth
Night*; "Where the bee sucks, there suck I" —*The Tempest*;
"What a candy deal of courtesy . . ." —*Henry IV, Part One*.)
Oscar Wilde's theory that the bard was homosexual, or
bisexual, is not as well-established as gay liberation writers
like to think—Shakespeare's actual imagery is virtually always heterosexual, as Eric Partridge demonstrates in
Shakespeare's Bawdy by simply listing all the sexual references
in the complete works. But, like Jesus, Shakespeare had so
strong a tender ("feminine") component that people who
identify masculinity with brutality are naturally inclined to
think he was queer. The nicknames recorded by his contemporaries—"Sweet Will" and "Gentle Will"—indicate rather clearly
that this bearded, bald-headed, chronically impoverished,
socially unacceptable and runt-sized son of a small-town
butcher was much closer, in type, to Allen Ginsberg than to
Ernest Hemingway. Nevertheless, he adored the ladies—
literally—and it seems more than a few of them adored him
in return. It is apt that Venus is the aggressive seducer of
Adonis in his long poem on that legend; men of this type
very often "play the waiting game" (as Kurt Weill called it in
September Song) and allowed the woman to make the advances. (If they are chess players, they will favor the "soft"
Reti or Alekhine openings instead of the aggressive center
games.) James Joyce even argued, on the basis of the sexual
imagery in the plays, that Anne Hathaway had seduced
Shakespeare; certainly, theirs was a slightly forced wedding,
the first child being born six months after the marriage
ceremony.

The bard's romanticism, which no English or American
poet has ever managed to escape catching to some degree,
comes right out of Eleanor's and Pierre Vidal's Sufi-
influenced sexual mysticism, as we have seen. Another influence, as Francis Yates has argued plausibly in *Giordano Bruno*

and the Hermetic Tradition, was the arch-heretic Bruno of Nola, burned at the stake in Rome in 1600. Bruno seems to have been the model for Berowne in Shakespeare's *Love's Labour's Lost.* He was in England around 1583–85 and his sonnet sequence, *De gli eroici furori,* published at Oxford in 1585, is a celebration of sexual love with interspersed prose passages relating these poems to the mystic quest for Unity (Freud's "oceanic experience"). Berowne's great speech in *Love's Labour's Lost*—

> For valour is not Love a Hercules
> Still climbing trees in the Hesperides?
> Subtle as Sphinx, as sweet and musical
> As bright Apollo's lute, strung with his hair;
> And when Love speaks, the voice of all the gods
> Make heaven drowsy with the harmony

—is not mere pretty language, as such things usually are in Shakespeare's countless imitators. It is a heretical statement, following Bruno's sonnets and the tradition of Eleanor of Aquitaine, bolding declaring the path of the lover superior to that of the soldier or the ascetic. As Francis Yates suggests, it is even possible that Prospero the Magician in *The Tempest* is also modeled on Bruno's magico-Hermetic practices, which involved quite a bit of the old Cathari-Templar-troubadour tradition of sexual occultism.

Ezra Pound, the modern poet who has given the most careful attention to historical research on the evolution of these notions, explains in somewhat guarded language (he was writing for the prudish English public in 1933): ·

> They [the troubadours] are opposed to a form of stupidity not limited to Europe, that is idiotic asceticism and a belief that the body is evil. . . .
> The senses at first seem to project a few yards beyond the body . . . [in] a decent climate where a man leaves his nerve-set open, or allows it to tune in to its ambience, rather than struggling, as a northern race has to for self-preservation, to

guard the body from assaults of weather. . . .

He declines, after a time, to limit reception to his solar plexus. The whole thing has nothing to do with taboos and bigotries. It is more than the simple athleticism of *mens sana in corpore sano*. The concept of the body as perfect instrument of the increasing intelligence pervades. . . .

We appear to have lost the radiant world where one thought cuts through another with clean edge, a world of moving energies . . . *magnetisisms that take form, that are seen, or that border the visible,* the matter of Dante's paradiso, the glass under water, the form that seems a form seen in a mirror, those realities perceptible to the sense . . . untouched by the two maladies, the Hebrew disease, the Hindoo disease, fanaticisms and excess that produce Savonarola. . . .[17]

John Donne, who may have influenced English romantic poetry almost as much as Shakespeare, attended Oxford while Bruno was lecturing there and seems to have picked up some of the Nolan's doctrines. The fact that Donne's poems often have double and triple meanings, concealed jokes and hidden symbolism is a critical commonplace, but this has not usually been related to the use of similar red herrings by the "Hermeticists" like Bruno who always sought to conceal their sexual teachings from the Holy Inquisition by such devices. In this connection, Donne's *The Ecstasy* is notable as a poem that has almost always been misunderstood by scholarly commentators. Here are the key stanzas, with emphasis added by me in the form of italics:

Where, like a pillow on a bed,
   A pregnant bank swell'd up to rest
The violet's reclining head,
   Sat we two, one another's best.
So t'intergraft our hands, as yet
   Was all the means to make us one,
   And pictures on our eyes to get
   Was all our propagation.

As 'twixt two equal armies fate
  Suspends uncertain victory,
Our souls, which to advance their state
  Were gone out, hung 'twixt her and me.

And whilst our souls negotiate there
  We *like sepulchral statues* lay;
Allday the same our postures were
  And we said nothing all the day.

This is generally described as an exemplar of "Platonic love," but it is almost certainly nothing of the kind. Readers unaware of the Tantric-Sufi tradition in Tibet, India and the Near East and its transmission through the Templar-troubadour cult and the various "alchemists" and Illuminati assume that if Donne and his lady *"sat"* together they must have been without sexual contact. Actually—see any Tibetan painting of the *yabyum* position, as it is called—sitting in each other's laps in the double-lotus position is basic in all sexual yoga. According to some writers there are neurological reasons for this—it allegedly diverts the sexual energy or bioelectricity from the central nervous system and sends it into the autonomic (involuntary) system—but, from a Freudian point of view, it restores the male to the *purely passive* role of the infant at the breast and thus represents the oralization of the genital embrace. Not unexpectly, the purpose of this is to recapture Freud's "oceanic experience" or the "trance of Unity" as mystics call it. In some traditions, influenced by Gnostic magic ideas, the couple stares into each other's eyes; cf. Donne's "and pictures in our eyes to get/Was all our propagation." This method is also a form of birth control, since it allows the male to experience orgasm without ejaculation. It was used for contraception in the anarcho-communist "free love" commune of the Bible Perfectionists of the famous Oneida Colony in upstate New York, circa 1840–1870. Contemporary Tantric teachers tell pupils to imitate the famous statues of the Black Temple near Benares—

the one with the erotic carvings—and seek a similar immobility; cf. Donne's "We like sepulchral statues lay." This position can be continued far longer than any other sexual pastime, the Baba Ram Dass may have been using it on the famous occasion when, under LSD, he remained in sexual ecstasy for hours and hours; cf. Donne's "All day the same our postures were."

As for Donne's claim about the souls leaving the bodies—well, ask anybody who has mastered this art. You will hear even more astonishing claims. Dr. Bergler's notion that the infant thinks the mother's breast is part of his own body may not be so fanciful, after all.[18]

It is remarkable that this poem has been mistaken for some ethereal or Platonic idealism. Donne's other poetry of that period is explicitly bawdy[19] and even here, in *The Ecstasy* itself, he ends by explicitly rejecting traditional spiritualization of the love relationship, saying:

> Love's mysteries in souls do grow,
>   *But yet the body is his book,*
>   [Italics mine]

Some readers, acknowledging that there is abundant evidence of a secret sexual-occult tradition in Europe from the Templars onward, will yet question that the Tibetan double-lotus sitting position was part of this. If Donne is not explicit enough, here is his contemporary, the "alchemist" Thomas Vaughan, hinting at the same secret teaching in his *Coelum Terrace* (1650) under the guise of discussing the "First Matter" or "Philosopher's Stone":

> The true furnace [where the "Matter" is "bathed"—R.A.W.] is a little simple shell; thou mayst easily carry it in one of thy hands. . . . As for the work itself, it is no way troublesome; a lady may . . . attend this philosophy without disturbing her fancy. For my part, I think women are fitter for it than men, for in such things they are more neat and patient, being used

to the small chemistry of sack-possets and other finical sugar-sops. . . .

But I had almost forgot to tell thee that which is all in all, and it is the greatest difficulty in all the art—namely, the fire. . . . The proportion and regime of it is very scrupulous, but the best rule to know it by is that of the Synod: "Let not the bird fly before the fowler." *Make it sit while you give fire,* and then you are sure of your prey. For a close I must tell thee that the philosophers call this fire their bath, but it is a bath of Nature, not an artificial one; for it is not of any kind of water. . . . In a word, without this bath nothing in the world is generated. . . . Our Matter is a most delicate substance and tender, like the animal sperm, for it is almost a living thing. Nay, in very truth, it hath some small portion of life. . . .

"Let him who is not familiar with Proteus have recourse to Pan."[20]

This is intended to baffle the ordinary reader, and it certainly succeeds. The "bird" is the sperm, which, when this method is successful, is deflected into he bladder rather than ejaculated (although Vaughan, like Bruno and the Oriental Tantrists, probably believed that it went up the spinal cord to the brain). The "work" is copulation without motion, in the sitting position. The confusing "fire" which is also a "bath" is the trance which results. The "matter" is again the sperm—note how neatly Vaughan conceals and reveals this. The reference to Proteus, god of transformations, and Pan, god of sexuality, is another hint. If the reader has not identified the "true furnace," let him consult Donne's *Love Alchemy*, where he will find:

And as no chemic yet th'elixir got
But glorifies his pregnant pot.

With this much background, the reader should now be able to grasp that the "extravagant metaphors" in love poets like Vidal, Sordello, Chaucer, Shakespeare, Donne, etc., are often not a matter of flattering the lady but serious statements of a philosophy which runs directly counter to the basic assumptions of our anal-patriarchal culture. Specifically, the repeated, perfectly clear identifications of the poet's mistress with a goddess are part of the mental set, or ritual, connected with this cult. Tibetan teachers train disciples of Tantra to think of the female partner as being literally, not metaphorically, the goddess Shakti, divine partner of Shiva. The Sufis, working within the monotheistic patriarchy of Islam, could not emulate this, but made her an angel communicating between Allah and man. The witch covens made her the great mother goddess. Aleister Crowley's secret teachings, in our own century, instructed his pupils to envision her as the Egyptian star-goddess, Nuit.

When anthropologist Weston La Barre says, "Mothers make magicians; fathers, gods," he means that the magic or shamanistic trance is a return to the bliss at the breast of the all-giving mother, while religion is an anal propitiation of a fearful god who is an enlarged portrait of the punishing father. These distinctions do not always remain sharp — Tantra managed to get incorporated into the patrist framework of Hinduism, and Sufi sex-magic into the equally patrist Moslem faith of Allah. In the West, however, patriarchy became extreme; Jehovah would bode no rivals, least of all a goddess equal to himself, and the magic-matriarchal-oral cults were driven underground, masqueraded as pseudosciences like alchemy, or came forth only in the form of poetry. Even so, patriarchy is so nervous of rivals in the West that the poet has come under considerable suspicion at many times, is often thought to be "queer" in one sense or another and, in the most anal cultures, often seems to be deliberately ignored or starved into submission. (If he is kind enough to die young, he is then forgiven and becomes a kind of secular Christ or martyr, as in the Dylan Thomas cult.) In England, the prejudice is so bad, Robert Graves notes in The White Goddess, that poets when forced to identify themselves—on government forms or in courtrooms, say—

will almost always use such terms as "teacher," "novelist," "historian" or whatever else they happen to be besides poets.

In *Mammon and the Black Goddess*, Graves nicely summarizes the relationship between poetry and the old oral cults of magic and matriarchy:

> The poet is, on the whole, anti-authoritarian, agoraphobic and intuitive rather than intellectual; but his judgments are coherent. Symptoms of the trance in which poetic composition occurs differ greatly from those of an induced mediumistic trance; though both seem directed by an external power. In a poetic trance, which happens no more predictably than a migraine or an epileptic fit, this power is traditionally identified with the ancient Muse-goddess. . . .
>
> Almost every poet has a personal Muse, a relationship first introduced into Europe from Sufi sources in Persia and Arabia during the early Middle Ages.

Poetry and magic, then, are based on a belief that thought can create its own reality—which Sir James Frazer in *The Golden Bough* called the theory of "the omnipotence of thought" and which Freud, in his comment on Frazer's anthropological investigations in *Totem and Taboo*, traced back to the child's power, with an outcry of desire, to make the missing mother mysteriously appear again and offer the all providing breast. It is no accident, then, that so many poems, from the *Odyssey* right up to Joyce's great prose-poem, *Finnegans Wake*, contain magical "invocations" summoning the goddess to appear at once.

We can now see that there might have been more than a joke in the famous exploit of Eleanor's father, Guillaume of Aquitaine, who built a private brothel or harem on his land in the exact architectural style of contemporary convents. The "convents" of the old matriarchal religions, of course, had been devoted to what is alternately called hierogamy or sacred prostitution or sex magic; perhaps Guillaume had been consciously trying to revive that. And when

Eleanor herself rode through Jerusalem with bared breasts,
she also may have been prompted by more than high spirits.
It is traditional in many schools of initiation to require some
such public act, which is thought to have magical significance
and also separates one sharply from the obedient servants
of the existing establishment. Parading those emblems of
matriarchal fertility-worship through the Holy Land of the
world's three strongest patriarchal religions—Judaism, Christianity and Islam—may have been an act of fealty to the old
mother goddess and an invocation attempting to restore her
worship.

If so, it has only been partially successful . . . thus far.

The taboo on showing the breast is certainly odd if one
considers it in relation to the attractive features of other
animals. One does not read of peacocks who are ashamed
of their gorgeous tail-feathers, of goldfish hiding their lovely
fiery-yellow markings, of lionesses having squeamish feelings about their brutal beauty. Yet a woman of today (unless
she is a professional topless dancer) might still go through
the processes which the psychologist Flugel described in
1930:

> A woman may, for example, refrain from going to a dance in
> a very *décolleté* dress: (a) Because, although she thinks it
> becomes her and she experiences a real gratification at the sight
> and feeling of her bare upper body, she yet experiences a sense
> of shame and embarrassment at the mere fact that she should
> do so. The modest impulse is here directed against desire. . . . .
> (b) Because, although she experiences none of the scruples
> just mentioned and freely enjoys the sight of herself in her
> mirror, she yet fears that she may unduly stimulate sexual
> desire in her prospective partners; in this case the modesty is
> still directed against desire, but now refers to feelings in others
> rather than to feelings in the self. (c) Because, on putting on
> the dress, she is immediately overcome by a feeling of revul-
> sion at her own image. . . . . Modesty here works against
> disgust aroused in her own mind. . . . . (d) Because, although
> she may be pleased at the effect of the low-cut dress, she thinks

of the shock that her appearance in it will cause to certain puritanically minded friends. . . . In this case, modesty is directed against disgust . . . in others rather than feelings in herself.[21]

Against this is the primordial desire to appear beautiful and fashionable.

Worse yet, the picture grows still more complex if the lady is married, for now she will consider her husband's wishes in the matter, as Flugel goes on to point out. The husband may wish her to dress daringly if he is relatively free of neurotic jealously and/or enjoys Veblen's "conspicuous consumption." Flaunting her breasts, then, is *his* way of showing other men what a prize he has captured. On the other hand, he may fear this as leading to dangerous competition. Judging by the way Arab women have traditionally been forced to dress, Arab men are particularly paranoid about such possibilities. In addition to these possible reactions, there is the complexity of "moral" squeamishness or its absence, this time in *his* head. Finally, there is the question of whether the lady is in a mood this particular night to please her husband or to annoy him. . . . .

And to cap off this pyramid of absurdities, the lady also has to stop and read the latest Supreme Court ruling before finally deciding. Eight old men and one lady she's never met personally will sit in solemn conclave and announce how many inches of her are decent this year and how many inches are diabolic and obscene. We can only conclude, as Flugel did, that attitudes toward clothing and the body are entirely dominated by irrationality.

Or as Mark Twain said: "Man is a fool, and woman, for tolerating him, is a damned fool."

[11] Berkeley, California, Rip-Off Press, 1970.

[12] Wolfgang Lederer, M.D., *The Fear of Women* (New York: Grune and Stratten, 1958).

[13] Martin Luther, for instance, had his peak religious experience in the privy. Later Lutheran theologians have tried to hide this fact, speaking of the room as the "tower," but Luther's own words are unambiguous; see Norman O. Brown's *Life Against Death.*

[14] G. Rattray Taylor, *Sex in History* (New York: Vanguard, 1955).

[15] St. Augustine, *The City of God* (New York: Modern Library, 1950).

[16] Taylor, *op. cit.,* p. 127.

[17] *Literary Essays of Ezra Pound* (New York: New Directions, n.d.). In *The Spirit of Romance,* with more clarity but equal caution, Pound grants that what was involved was a yoga utilizing "the opposite polarities of male and female." De Rougemont in *Love in the Western World* leaves no doubt that it was classic Tantric yoga, prolonging the sex act into a trance in which the "souls" or "magnetisms" are, to some degree, visible.

[18] See the accounts of people who under the influence of marijuana could not tell what was their own body and what was their lover's, in my *Sex and Drugs: A Journey Beyond Limits* (Las Vegas: Falcon Press, 1986).

[19] Here are a few tender verses from his *To His Mistress Going To Bed*:

> Your gown's going off, such beauteous state reveals
> As when as when from Flow'ry meads the hills shadow steals.
> Off with your wiry coronet and show
> The hairy diadem which on you doth grow.
>
> License my roving hands and let them go
> Behind, before, above, between, below.
>
> To teach thee, I am naked first. Why then
> What need'st thou have more covering than a man?

[20] A. E. Waits, ed., *The Works of Thomas Vaughan, Mystic and Alchemist* (New Hyde Park: University Books, 1968).

[21] J. C. Flugel, *The Psychology of Clothes* (New York: International Universities Press, 1930).

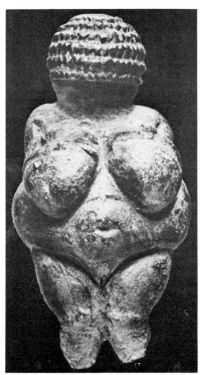

Photo courtesy of the Bettman Archive

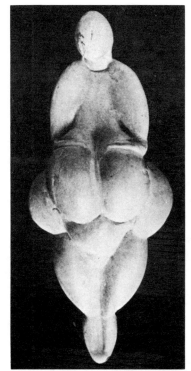

Photo courtesy of the Bettman Archive

Photo courtesy of the Bettman Archive

Photo courtesy of the Bettman Archive

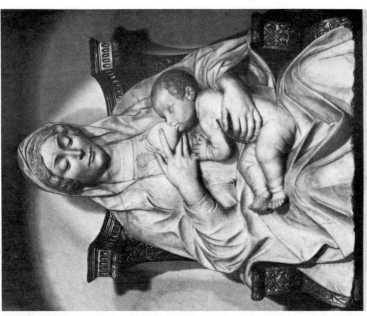

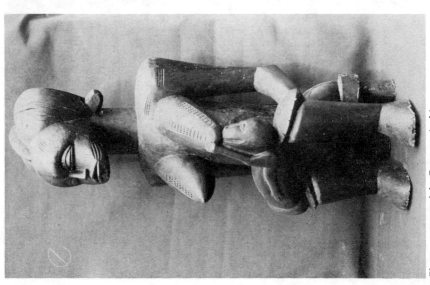

Photo courtesy of the Bettman Archive

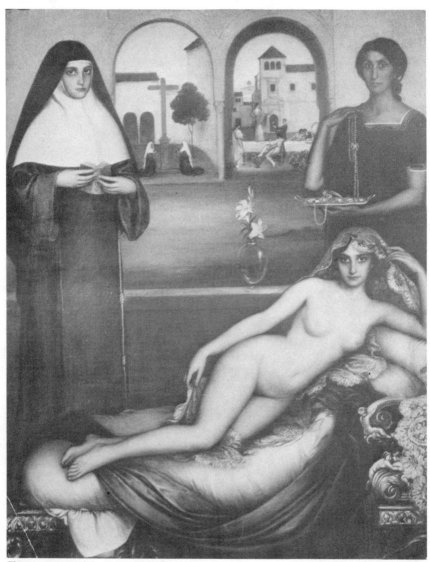

Photo courtesy of the Bettman Archive

Photo courtesy of the Bettman Archive

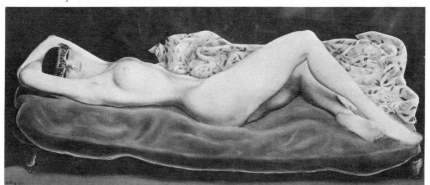

Photo courtesy of the Bettman Archive

Photo courtesy of the Bettman Archive

Photo courtesy of the Bettman Archive

Photo courtesy of the Bettman Archive

Photo courtesy of the Bettman Archive

Photo courtesy of the Bettman Archive

Photo courtesy of the Bettman Archive

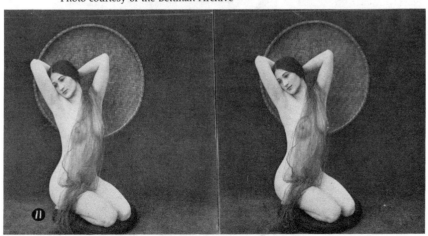

Photo courtesy of the Bettman Archive

Clara Bow

original "IT" girl of the

Photo courtesy of the Bettman Archive

Photo courtesy of the Bettman Archive

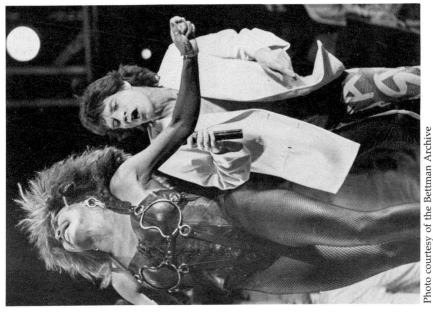

Photo courtesy of the Bettman Archive

Photo by Harry Widoff. Copyright © 1989 Harry Widoff.

5. The return of the repressed

. . .under purple canopies
With mighty-breasted mistresses
Magnificent as lionesses—
Tender and terrible caresses[22]—
— Aleister Crowley, *Aha!*

As Timothy Leary has pointed out in *Psychology Today* (Vol. 6, No. 8, January 1973), repression has so molded the character of Christian and post-Christian civilization that even our psychologists have not studied hedonistic behavior in depth. We know a great deal (perhaps more than is safe to know) about conditioned behavior and how the proper scheduling of reward and punishment can persuade a pigeon to stand with his head under his wing when he wants to be fed (B. F. Skinner has accomplished this feat) and how similar techniques can persuade a man to confess to crimes he hasn't committed (the Russians are reputed to know a lot about that). Unconditioned or hedonistic behavior, however, has hardly been examined at all; Dr. Skinner very bluntly declares that he doubts such behavior exists at all. With a few exceptions, the psychologists and psychiatrists who admit that unconditioned behavior exists are quite firmly attached to the opinion that it is always pathological or abnormal.

Not unexpectedly, sexual behavior (which often seems unconditioned and certainly moves rapidly into the area of pure hedonism after a certain "point of no return" which we all intuitively recognize) was the last behavior to be studied scientifically. For reasons that are perhaps far from mysterious, the first approach came through the study of the hysterical and insane, as pioneered by the great Charcot in Paris in the late 19th Century. Charcot's famous conclusion that these symptoms "are always sexual—always—always—always"[23] seems to have been regarded as a *Dummheit* by most of his pupils. But as we all know, one young Viennese named Freud took the old man seriously and began examining his own hysteric patients more closely to see if this wild hypothesis might be correct. We generally forget Freud's subsequent disillusionment when, in spite of all the evidence he collected that Charcot was right, other evidence mounted up to convince him that such symptoms actually derived from traumatic childhood and infantile experiences. Since everybody knew that children and infants have no sexual drive, Charcot must have been wrong. . . .

Freud bogged down at that point for several months before an even wilder theory occurred to him: Children and infants are sexual beings, after all. Of course, he hesitated a long time before daring to publish such a crazy notion—and when he did, the majority of the medical men pronounced solemnly that he must have been driven loony by association with his disturbed patients. Today, when even Freud's harshest critics (even the women's liberation writers who have revived the notion that he was Satan incarnate) admit that infant sexuality exists, it is hard to us to remember how invisible this was to his contemporaries or how hard it was for him himself to see it at first. **It is, of course, even harder for us to think that there might be equally important facts about human life that are equally invisible to us because of our own socially given dogmas. . . .**

And a more interesting point: Trying to explain the so-called actual neuroses (nervous twitches, anxiety, dizzy spells, mild hysterias) Freud found sufficient differences between them and the psychoneurosis to posit an alternative theory about their origin. He decided they were *caused by excessive masturbation.* (No, that is not a misprint.) Of course, virtually every medical authority of his time believed the same thing, and the fear of falling prey to such illnesses from overfrequent onanism led to many ridiculous extremes, such as a "male chastity belt," patented in the United States in the 1890s, which had a hole to allow the penis to pass through for urination but also had a ring of needle-sharp points around the hole to stab the organ if it became large enough for handling or cuddling. Fathers apparently bought this remarkable device and put it on their teen-age sons—"for their own good," of course.

In 1812, Dr. Benjamin Rush, generally credited as the father of modern psychiatry, declared that masturbation in the male "produces seminal weakness, impotence, dysury, tabes dorsalis, pulmonary consumption, dypepsia, dimness of sight, vertigo, epilepsy, hypochondriasis, loss of memory, manalgia, fatuity and *death*." Within twenty years masturbation was generally accepted as a *cause* of insanity. As recently as 1938 psychoanalyst Karl Menninger wrote that in the "unconscious mind [masturbation] always represents aggression against someone."

If Freud shared the masturbation hysteria of his time, nobody else was eager to push sexual knowledge beyond the point at which he left it. The obvious step was to begin with taxonomy and classification, the usual procedure in a new science. Aside from small-scale investigations by Freud's contemporaries Krafft-Ebing and Havelock Ellis, this next step was not taken. Decade followed decade and nobody had the impetus to fill the vacuum; perhaps the slander heaped on Freud's head discouraged other pioneers. Finally, in the 1940s, Kinsey published a sampling of human sexual behavior large enough to have scientific significance. We had already learned (if we cared to look in the right books) all about the sexual patterns of the robin and the crow, the elephant and the whale, the worm and the amoeba; now at last we knew something about ourselves. Those who were then mature, or at least adolescent, will remember that the universal reaction was, "My God, I'm not the only one who does that!"

We still had to wait until the late 1960s for accurate data about the physiology of orgasm to be gathered by Masters and Johnson.

Leary is obviously right: The fear of hedonistic behavior is still intense in this civilization. The anal mentality, sternly (or anxiously) wedded to willpower, logic and strict control still prevails and still has a phobic terror of spontaneous body processes or anything soft and oral.

Consider the splendid photograph on page 000. To a normal person whose oral and anal stages were passed without trauma or "sticking," this is quite lovely and no more need be said about it. To a cathected oral type, it is, on the contrary, an almost religious vision provoking either deep grief or wild joy, depending on how close he is to having turned his whole universe into the cosmic lover-provider of which this reminds him. And to an anal personality, this is shocking, improper, "dirty," "smutty" and devilish.

Thus when the breast began to stage a comeback after the great denial of the 1920s, it appeared in a way calculated to look, or almost look, "accidental." This was the age of the sweater girl, typified by the early publicity photos of Lana Turner and Paulette Goddard. At first, these ladies never showed any cleavage, and the breasts were covered as thoroughly as any prude could possibly demand. If the breasts, nevertheless, dominated the photograph—well, it could be argued, that was only nature's fault. The ladies just happened to be built that way. Skeptics in the pulpit who insisted that the sweaters were deliberately tight in order to emphasize this feature could be accused of having "dirty minds," thereby turning the anality of the prudes back against themselves. "Joy was it in that dawn to be alive." The Turner-Goddard look was copied everywhere, and the oral types had millions of lovely breasts to ogle on all sides, while the anal types could not complain that *flesh* was being exposed. The sweater girl emphasized her mammalian signaling equipment in a most conspicuous way but showed none of the cleavage visible in the evening gowns of even the uptight Victorian Era.

Paulette Goddard even managed to embody the goddess rather conspicuously in her quite public "private" life by taking a world cruise on Charlie Chaplin's yacht while—horrors—not legally wed to him. Moralists fumed and with typical anal resentment added this to their long list of grudges against poor Chaplin, which finally led to his quasi-voluntary exile from the United States. Miss Goddard went on to become one of top sex-stars of the 1940s and its most talented comedienne. Although overshadowed by Chaplin's genius when co-starring with him, she quite often managed to steal the laughs (as well as the lusts) of the audience when paired with lighter-weight comics like Bob Hope. Not until Stella Stevens did we see another comedienne of equal sexual allure. It is even possible to consider the return of the breast under Miss Goddard's aegis as, in a small way, a turning point in American cultural history comparable to the bare-breasted ride of Eleanor of Aquitaine through Jerusalem.

It must be admitted that, once rediscovered, the breast became almost an obsession with Americans—one which provoked much overt amusement (and possibly come covert envy) in foreign visitors. It was soon proclaimed by all observers aspiring to intellectual status that the "mammary preoccupation" of Americans showed that we were an "infantile" society compared to the presumably more "mature" continentals. Nobody at the time (so great was the national inferiority complex, at least among the classes who engage in such debate) asked if the Spanish preoccupation with sexual blasphemy[24], the Byzantine prudery of the Russians, the strange fascination with coprophilia visible in German erotica (and in the Nazis' anti-Semitic rantings), the buttock-and-cane hang-up of the English, etc., were really more wholesome. It was soberly proclaimed that this breast-obsession indicated a deep American aversion for the vagina. Nobody dared to quote the rising birthrate as an answer to that absurdity. We were all trained to think of ourselves as uncivilized bumpkins and to look across the Atlantic for enlightenment (as young people today are looking across the Pacific). The attitude had been around since before the Revolution, and Francis Hopkinson, the lyric poet who also signed the Declaration of Independence, once complained in a diatribe against Europe:

> Can we never be thought
> To have learning or grace
> Unless it be brought
> From that damnable place?

In fact, the American breast craze of the late 1930s–1950s is probably best explained on *nutritional* grounds. In those years, little girls in America were being better fed and got more vitamins than little girls in Europe; at that time there were not many large, rounded breasts in Europe for European men to get excited over. As soon as the postwar recovery began in Europe, some really dazzling bosoms appeared on such lovelies as Gina Lollabrigida, Sophia Loren and Anita Ekberg, and European men were quick to show a quite "Americanized" appreciation of them. And why not? As we made abundantly clear earlier, breast worship was scarcely an American invention; it dates back at least to the Venus of Willendorf.

Of course, there is real breast-fetishism in America (as there is everywhere). Some men are attached to large breasts as stickily as other fetishists are to undergarments, shoes or leather. People in the porno business know this and appeal to it in their ads—as, for instance:

> A 20-year-old Irish girl with the mostest—her bust is all of 47 inches—photographed in Full Nude positions that will be sure to please . . .[25]

On the other hand, some men prefer petite breasts and

would regard a 47-inch bust as a bit too much, almost a comic effect. I once worked on a men's magazine (not PLAYBOY) in which the girls were always small-breasted, almost boyish; I though this was the publisher's personal eccentricity until he directly ordered me to "print some chicks with meat on their bones, fa' Christ sake!" It turned out that previous issues had mirrored the prejudices of the editor immediately before me, who later emerged as a leading spokesman for the Gay Liberation Movement.

(All men who like large breasts are *not* fetishists; all men who like small breasts are *not* gay. *Freudian theories become science fiction when they are considered laws applying to all rather than just statistical generalizations applying to many.*)

It must be admitted that Hollywood, which could be considered the capital of the breast culture in those years, proceeded with quite a schizophrenic air for a long time, especially after the novelty of the sweater girl fad wore off and it became obvious that men wanted to see some flesh. The Catholic hierarchy was still powerful in those days, and this group of celibate old men in black skirts had some very strange attitudes by anybody's standards (unless you also happened to be a celibate old man who liked to wear black skirts). One of the pleasures of looking at 1940s and early 1950s movies on the Late Show is watching how the cameraman and director collaborate to make every inch of cleavage look like—in the Zen Buddhist phrase—a *happy accident.* "Oh, no," they always seem to be saying, "we didn't set this shot up to expose as much as possible of the leading lady's globes. She just happened to be sitting down wearing a low-cut evening gown while the camera moved overhead to show you the butler bringing in the drinks." The camera, in those days, always moved past such a tempting sight without pausing, just as the eyes of boys in Catholic schools are supposed to move. When it first began to linger, in the early 1950s, the sexual revolution was beginning.

The excuses introduced for getting the leading lady

partly undressed, in those days, were worthy of the casuistry of the Jesuits (since they had to pass the scrutiny of the Jesuits). It seems, looking at these films on TV, that Americans in the epoch spent most of their time getting ready for bed (where they slept alone, even if legally married. Twin beds were introduced if the leading man was playing the husband of the leading lady). Ladies were always getting caught in rainstorms (necessitating a change of clothing) in those days, too; and if there was a phone call in the plot, you could be sure Betty Grable or Jennifer Jones or whoever would have to get out of the bathtub to answer it.

In this hypocritical context, with every inch of flesh seeming to appear only by *happy accident*, the breast naturally dominated the genitalia, because the censors could agree that a few inches of cleavage might have just slipped by in the "natural course of things" if the actress were wearing an evening gown or a bathing suit or a nightie. But if a few inches of crotch were showing, well, by God, this was *contrived* and even *prurient* and probably downright *dirty*, and there was no doubt at all what Cardinal Spellman would say about it. That worthy gentleman, later elevated from cardinal to hawk by embittered Catholic pacifists for his enthusiastic support of the Vietnam War, had already let all and sundry know that Jane Russell's cleavage, as revealed in *The Outlaw*, did not seem like a happy accident at all but a conscious attempt to make male moviegoers feel *horny* and thereby lead them into sin. The argument that Miss Russell just happened to be built that way cut no ice with *him*; and he seemed definitely inclined to the view that if such was her anatomical endowment then the producers should bloody well garb her to conceal God's mistake and prevent the men in the audience from gawking like tourists at the Grand Canyon whenever she leaned forward. And then Jayne Mansfield appeared, with an even more striking front elevation than La Russell and it was obvious that in anything less concealing than concrete she would still incite prurient and lustful thoughts and be an occasion of sin. Nothing short of an amputation would alleviate the situation in this case, and the hierarchy did not retain enough power to force Miss Mansfield to submit to surgery. Of course, she did eventually die in a freak auto accident that decapitated her, and believers in Charles Fort's theory of unconscious witchcraft might hint that the bad vibes of mammalophobes had finally caught up with her.

By the early 1960s, the demands of the European market had induced a situation in which some Hollywood studios were shooting two versions of certain scenes: one in which only part of the bosom was revealed (for American audiences) and another in which the whole beautiful spectacle was shown in its naked glory, nipples and all (yum-yum— but only for the continent). When this practice became public knowledge, and PLAYBOY magazine meanwhile was showing some extraordinarily lovely breasts in every issue, the end of the Catholic hegemony over our cinema was in sight. Men began to ask if the church was all that powerful in our supposedly pluralistic society and if everything adults were allowed to see had to acquire the Vatican Seal of Approval first. Producers wanted to show what the public wanted to see, and the public wanted to see as much as the producers dared to show. It became absurd that a minority of males who had renounced their own manhood could set standards which 130,000,000 non-Catholics must then obey. Where had Jeffersons' "wall of separation between church and state" disappeared to? The Vatican had flown over it like the Nazis jumping the Maginot Line and landing in Paris. The wall was firmly set back in place and long last adult movies began to appear in the United States just as if we were, after all, the pluralistic secular society the Founding Fathers had intended.

Nonetheless, the first time I saw a nipple in an American movie, I was jarred. It was as if I had acquired a part-time schizophrenia which only went into operation on entering a movie theater. Women, of course, had nipples in real life, in PLAYBOY, in European movies, in pornography, in the *National Geographic*; but in Hollywood, I had been trained to half-believe, they had all been born with a piece of fabric that could never be removed, not even by the greatest surgeon in the cosmos. And yet here they were on the screen; it was *Hawaii*, and the bare bosoms were well-justified—oh, very carefully justified—by historical accuracy, and yet I remembered when Cardinal Richelieu had mysteriously changed to Prime Minister Richelieu (in the Gene Kelly version of *The Three Musketeers*) to avoid offending papist pride, just as history changed in *1984* to save the party's credibility. (And how many times had we seen actors who were notorious rakes and actresses who were renowned for randiness playing Roman or Greek pagans or even pirates yet still compelled to speak dialogue that had been tailored to sound as if they had been raised in Catholic convents, as if—and this was the great unspoken myth in all American movies until the mid 1960s—*everybody everywhere* had been raised in convents, and nobody had ever doubted the peculiar sexual notions of the Council of Cardinals?) And yet there were nipples, real live nipples on the screen, and I knew that an era had ended. It was like Roosevelt's death when I was 13; until then I had half-believed that there *would never be* another president. Until those nipples appeared in *Hawaii*, I thought I would never see an American movie that wasn't implicitly a Roman Catholic movie.

Of course, the Catholic hierarchy had been intelligent (and, by their own lights, right) all along: Repression is never a static process, but must always be dynamic, either moving forward toward total control or retreating backward as the floodgates open to that force which French intellectuals quite correctly capitalize: Desire. Shakespeare asked how Beauty could survive, being no stronger than a flower, and Tennessee Williams answered (in *Camino Real*) that the flowers in the mountains always break through the rocks. The cry of

"Flower Power" in the 1960s might as well have been *Nipple Power*: Once those gentle buds had crashed through the rocks of repression, Desire was free and the walls of the cities began to shake. Real language began to be heard on the screens of movie houses; other parts of the body, one by one, crept out the darkness of shame and concealment; topless clubs appeared with bottomless clubs soon after; Blacks rebelled against poverty, students against monotony, even straight citizens raised their voices against a war that made no sense (but when had straight citizens ever objected to a war on *those* grounds before?); the Indians emerged from the depression that had crushed them since their last defeat at Wounded Knee and began to agitate again; eventually there were mutinies in prisons, in armies, on ships, even among Air Force officers. In Frederick Perls's terminology, people had stopped harboring their *resentments* and began to make *demands*—and a large number of them were proclaiming, in loud voices, that they would use *any means necessary* to get what they wanted. By the end of the decade, the Jesus Freaks, the women's liberationists and the silent majority were all in a panic, trying desperately to rebuild at least some of the walls of repression which traditionally have kept civilized humanity from attempting to *immanentize the eschaton*. This phrase is from conservative historian Kurt Vogelin and refers, in technical theological language, to the heresy of the Gnostics, who wished to produce heaven on this earth instead of postponing it until after death. Vogelin says this heresy underlies all forms of radicalism and rebellion, and he is probably right. Modern history is a war between Authority and Desire, and if Authority must demand submission, Desire will settle for nothing less than the attainment of its gratification.

We have even reached the point where serious scholarly folk *with degrees after their names*, O my brothers—philosopher Herbert Marcuse in *Eros and Civilization*, classicist Norman O. Brown in *Life Against Death*—are turning Freudian weapons against Freud. Specifically, the Viennese sage's formula of reality principle and pleasure principle had assumed an eternal dialectic between these forces, pleasure ever urging us to seek instant gratification, reality always warning us to consider consequences before taking risks. This is certainly sane, and beyond dispute; but Freud had slipped in some dubious qualifications and limitations when we weren't looking. His reality principle turned out to include a great deal of repression that could not be justified by any real dangers at all, except the discomfort of colliding with Freud's own remnants of a Victorian superego. Masturbation, for instance, does no objective harm; adultery, which admittedly can lead to fist-fights or even murder in some cases, is neutral in others and most certainly has been beneficial at times; homosexuality is dangerous only with AIDS and without condoms. How much reality principle is there in the repression that permeates every day of every life in this civilization?

This, of course, is the heart of the Consciousness III debate. Charles Reich's *The Greening of America* became a runaway best seller—despite the fact that the majority of reviews were bitterly hostile—because Reich articulated what many other have hoped (or feared) was coming to pass; his Consciousness III is the renaissance of all the oral, tender, matrist values repressed for 3000 years in the Western World. Like McLuhan with his electronic mysticism, like Leary with his Acid Zen ("You are God. Remember?"), like Brown and Marcuse with their concept of freedom unlimited, Reich is important whether he is right or not. He has defined that sense of vertigo which all of us experienced as the 1960s taught us again and again that many things we thought eternal are likely to pass away before our eyes. The very venom found in criticisms of Reich (and of Brown, Marcuse, Leary and McLuhan) indicates that the critics themselves have a deep repressed fear that these heretics might be right after all.

Here, for instance, is a typical women's lib assault on Reich, from Nancy R. McWilliams in *The Con III Controversy*:

> To me, male chauvinism in the guise of undiluted love for all humanity, liberated sensuality, and spontaneous self-realization is far more insidious than anything Norman Mailer or Lionel Tiger represents. Further, it suggests a crazy vision of what human psychology or the self could be, what love is, what sex is, and what kinds of communities could allow for the wisdom and fulfillment that Reich so greatly values. . . . What kind of love is it that is diluted as to include all humanity indiscriminately, tolerating terror and suffering with the equanimity of a psychopath? It is possible that we will all drown in Reich's great chicken-soup of *Eros*.[26]

In a similar vein, a writer for the conservative *National Review* once wrote that the three most dangerous men in America were *not* Huey Newton of the Black Panther party, *not* any of the Communists or socialists or anarchists, *not* even any of the old-line hard-core pacifists like Dave Dellinger, but—guess who?—Timothy Leary, Marshall McLuhan and Norman O. Brown. How Charles Reich missed getting on that list is anybody's guess; he obviously belongs there. *Think of your Desires as Realities*, a slogan of the French student rebellion of 1968, is the underlying message of all four writers, the cause of the messianic hopes of their admirers and the cause also of the terror quite visible in their critics. Our whole civilization had been traditionally based on the reverse theorem: *Think of your Desires as Impossible*. Adjust. Conform. Accept. Submit.

Leslie Fiedler, a very distinguished literary critic who was later arrested (rightly or wrongly) for allowing young people to smoke marijuana in his living room, once wrote a sparkling little essay on obscenity in which he argued that every little boy who writes "Fuck You" on a fence is trying to enlarge reality to allow Desire a bit of living space. There is no doubt that Freud's classic formulation of the reality principle *assumed* a great deal about things which, having never been challenged, have never had to prove themselves. Now they are being challenged, and the polemics against challengers ("soft-headed" was the usual charge against the Reich; "incoherent," he shared with McLuhan; "cultist" was reserved for Leary; "bizarre," for some reason, is mostly reserved for Brown) suggest that the would-be defenders aren't quite sure where to begin.

For instance, the "filthy speech" movement at Berkeley—which began, after the more traditionally political "free speech" fight over the right of radicals to propagandize in certain previously restricted areas of the campus—commenced when some anonymous chap showed up at a rally with a placard bearing the legend

FUCK

(IF THIS SAID "KILL" I WOULDN'T GET ARRESTED)

Lenny Bruce, of course, was constantly being arrested for similar devices in his satirical nightclub act. When this movement caught on, and students were being arrested on all sides, the debate that followed was a marvel of incoherence; it was obvious that neither side could begin to fathom what the other side believed. If the battle for nudity on the screen had taken place more or less inarticulately, with neither side ever really defining the issue that split them, the "filthy speech" movement certainly did define the issue, or tried to. Nonetheless, the two sides still did not understand each other.

"Are these nipples dirty?" Lenny used to ask his audience, holding up a centerfold from PLAYBOY. "I think she's a very pretty lady," he would add naively, "and look at those lilacs on the shelf behind her, *mmm-mmm*. This is dirty?" Some people would laugh and cheer loudly; others would stomp out of the club in indignation. They would ask later, in genuine pain and confusion, "Why does he have to *stoop so low* to get a laugh?" They asked again, about the kids at Berkeley, "Why do they have to use those nasty words?"

The issue, of course, has nothing to do with logic. It is ridiculously easy to mock the fears of those who imagined Western civilization was threatened by Jane Russell's cleavage in the 1940s, or those who trembled at the absolutely bare breast of the Marilyn Monroe calendar in the 1950s, or those who felt that Lenny Bruce's saying "cocksucker" on stage in the early 1960s represented so clear and present a danger that he had to be locked up at once. On the other hand, cultural changes do come in clusters, and if naked breasts don't cause Indians to seize government offices or high officials to release confidential data to the press, the breasts are part of the pattern that indicates such changes are on the way. After all, a single moment of truth can break up decades of skillful pretensions. Look at Lenny Bruce in action:

Since all the moralists and purists support Las Vegas as the entertainment capital of the world, one would assume that the attraction at The Star Dust is *The Passion Play* or a Monet exhibit or the New York City Ballet with Eugene Ormandy conducting. But, no; what *is* the big attraction?

"Tits and ass."

I beg your pardon?

"Tits and ass," that's what the attraction is."

Just tits and ass?

"No, an apache team in between for rationalization."

Well, that must be just one hotel—what's the second big attraction?

"More tits and ass."

And the third?

"That's it, tits and ass, and more tits and ass."

Do you mean to tell me that *Life* magazine would devote three full pages to tits and ass?

"Yes, right next to the articles by Billy Graham and Norman Vincent Peale."

Well, that may be the truth, but you just can't put "Tits

and Ass" up on a marquee.

"Why not?"

Because it's dirty and vulgar, that's why.

"Titties are dirty and vulgar?"

No, you're not gonna bait me, it's not the titties, it's the words, it's the way you relate them. You can't have these words where kids can see them.

"Didn't your kid ever see a titty?"

I'm telling you, it's the words.

"I don't believe you. I believe, to you, it's the titty that's dirty, because I'll change the words to 'Tuchuses and Nay-nays Nightly!' "

That's a little better.

"Well, that's interesting. You're not anti-Semitic idiomatic, you're anti-Anglo-Saxon idiomatic. Then why don't we get really austere? Latin: 'Gluteus maximus and Pectorales majores Nightly!' "

Now, that's clean.

"To you, schmuck—but it's dirty to the Latins!"

"La Parisienne—The Follies—class with ass—French tits and ass—that's art! And if we don't make any more money with that you can have a Japanese nude show that absolves us both politically and spiritually, because who but a dirty Jap would show their keister? And we'll get the Norman Luboff choir to sing Remember Pearl Harbor. And then, if we don't make any more money with that, we'll combine the contemporary and the patriotic: American tits and ass. Grandma Moses tits and Norman Rockwell's ass . . ."

(Draw my ass. If you can draw my ass, you can draw. My ass, you can draw.)

Soon they will have just a big nipple up on the marquee, and maybe that's why you want to have FOR ADULTS ONLY because you're ashamed to tell your kids that you're selling and exploiting and making an erotic thing out of your mother's breast that gave you life.[27]

After 45 minutes of this sort of Gestalt free-association (a projection outward of Bruce's interval top dog and under dog) the average audience was weak from more than just laughter. They had been angry, and sorrowful, and guilty, and ready to cry a few times between the laughs, and they were no longer quite sure what they felt or believed about tits. Of all the voices attacking conformity in the 1960s, Bruce was the only one literally hounded to death, because repression can survive literally anything except a room full of people laughing at it.

---

[22] *The Equinox*, Vol. L, No. 3, 1910.

[23] *"C'est toujours la chose genital, toujours—toujours—toujours!"*

[24] Spanish pornography virtually always includes a scene in which the heroine is deflowered on an alter, under a crucifix or in a cemetery. Expurgated versions of the same theme reappear constantly in Spanish and Mexican comic books and "romantic" novels.

[25] Quoted in Sara Harris, *The Puritan Jungle: America's Sexual Underground* (New York: G.P. Putnam, 1969).

[26] Nancy R. McWilliams, "Reich and Women," in Philip Noble, ed., *The Con III Controversy* (New York: Pocket Books, 1971).

[27] Lenny Bruce, *How to Talk Dirty and Influence People* (New York: Playboy Press, 1965).

6. The breast expressed and the breast possessed

> The Polynesians, normally so vocal among themselves about sexual matters, are unwilling to talk at length with a European about erotica. This ad hoc modesty can also be seen in the behavior of some older women who cover their breasts when the European doctor arrives, although they usually go about without any upper garment.
> —Donald Marshall, *Ra'ivavae*[28]

A friend of mine once saw blue rays coming out of his girl friend's nipples. He was tripping on LSD at the time.

"An interesting hallucination," I ventured when he told me about this.

"I'm not so sure," he replied.

Well, we're certainly not going to take him seriously; we all know that acid heads are likely to believe *anything*. Even if the Russian parapsychologists claim to have repeatedly photographed an aura around the human body; even if Wilhelm Reich thought he could detect that aura with a modified telescope which he called an orgonoscope. No, we have already chanced some bizarre speculations and we are not going to rear up our membership card in the intellectual's guild entirely and rush forward to join the occultists. Not yet.

But it is interesting to compare this to the experience of theologian Alan Watts, who, in a legal LSD experiment ten years ago, saw strange rays in the sky, beyond a certain hill, and went the next day to look at the other side of that hill and found a radar installation. Shall we be bold enough to entertain even for a moment that hypothesis that LSD enabled Dr. Watts to see the normally invisible radar waves? Probably it is still safest to be respectable and ignore such speculations, even if a little devil inside urges us to quote, in this connection, from Patrick Trevor-Roper's *The World Through Blunted Sight*:

> Mescaline and other hallucinogenic drugs seem to cause an interruption of the "association fibres" in the posterior lobe of the brain, which mold the unconscious, cerebral image of the seen world into the conscious percept, *altering it, in the light of our experience and needs*, so that it falls into line with our established schemas, with all the attributes that we think proper for the object we now recognize. Mescaline thus allows us to see *a far truer image* than the ordered stereotype that our association fibres normally permit us to apprehend. It lets us see the true shadow-colors—the blue shadow in the snow, the green beneath the red object, and so on. . . . [Italics mine.]

But this is going far out. We will soon find ourselves in company with William Blake, the artist-poet who talked to the Old Testament prophets and saw angels; batty Blake, greatest of our lyric poets but certainly the last man to trust about the question of what is real—he who said, "The fool sees not the same tree that the wise man sees." (Did his trees look like Van Gogh's, or even wilder?) Certainly, we have found reasons to believe that Freud's oral type sees not the same breasts as the anal type, but what sort of man sees blue rays coming out of nipples? To ask is to answer: The same sort who sees halos around heads. No, we shall not go any further down that very murky road. Let us give Blake one last word and then pass him by. "The Head Sublime," he once wrote, "the heart Pathos, the genitals Beauty, the hands and feet Proportion." We will nod our heads in wry agreement with the wistful comment of science-fiction writer Carol Emshwiller: "It would be nice to live in a society where the genitals were really considered Beauty." Yes, Carol, it would.

It would be nice also to live in a society where the breasts were considered Beauty, where the act of love was considered lovely, where the word "fuck" was not considered more repulsive than the word "kill"—yes, for some of us, that would be nice, but for others it would be the end of the world, the whole world, the only world they have ever known. And this, really—just this and not the angels of Blake, the souls of Donne, the magnetisms of Pound, the rays of my acid-tripping friend—this mind-bender and ball-breaker of an epistemological enigma is what divides our society schismatically and schizophrenically and schizogenically, so that if one of us opens a topless bar, one hundred will come to patronize it and ten others will petition to have it closed down by the law. Mammalotry versus mammalphobia. The cannibal and the Christian, Dionysus and Apollo, the yogi and the commissar, "a tale told of Shem and Shaun," Yes I will versus no you can't. . . . On just so sharp a dagger is the heart lacerated and cut, and cut again and again, every day in 2000 years, and the resulting agony is called civilization. Or so says the savage inside, still fighting to get out.

These women on the island of Ra'ivavae, mentioned in the lead to this chapter: What do they think, rushing to grab a piece of cloth and cover their tits when "the European doctor" arrives? Are they suddenly ashamed of their nakedness, or are they humoring a man they regard as a lunatic? Probably both: We believe what we do, even when we disbelieve it, and this is the schizophrenia implicit in every act of submission to an authority that we fear more than we love. "We are all better artists than we know," Nietzsche said once, but he was not flattering us, he was talking about our capacity for self-deception. Watch people change everything from their posture to their awareness of reality when the boss walks through the office and you will know everything Nietzsche, or Freud or any other profound student of humanity had to teach. We are all Polynesians and we all cover up nervously when the European doctor passes by. Perhaps the only difference is that some of us trust him more of the time and some of us trust ourselves more of the time.

Certainly, the extent of the breast taboo in our anal culture is so extreme as to have influenced language also. We can scarcely talk about breasts in any idiom that is understood throughout the society. (According to H. Allen Smith, in *Mr. Klein's Kampf*, workers in brassiere factories have a slang of their own, to describe various sizes, from "peaches" up to "watermelons", but this is humorously grotesque rather then accurate, and is not generally known.) We have a full, rich and even poetic vocabulary to describe a lovely woman's face—hair like the Kansas cornfields, eyes as blue as Murphy's overalls, a fine upstanding Roman nose, full sensual lips, a determined little chin, and so on and so forth, with a whole silo of clichés which every lazy writer can count on to create the approximate image he wants in the reader's head. When it comes to breasts we can't say much more than "fairly big" or "fairly small," perhaps adding "kinda high" or "sorta sagging." Sara Reidman, writing in *Sexology* magazine in 1956, proposed a roughly scientific classification of four main types of breasts—conic, discoid, hemispheric and elongated—but this is scarcely known even by other sexologists. Again, compare the richness of our vocabulary for just one small part of the face, namely the nose. Everybody knows what a writer means when he refers to a Roman nose, a Jewish nose, a pug nose, a Durante schnozzola, a turned-up nose, a smashed-in boxer's nose, a cute little button nose, a snooty nose, etc. Conan Doyle's "hawklike" label for Sherlock Holmes's beak has so impressed itself on readers that no actor with an average-size or smaller probiscus has ever dared to play the part. But that is above the chin. From the neck down our language suggests that the lights went out with the arrival of St. Paul on the scene and we haven't been able to see each other since then.

Actually, in spite of our not having a clear language

about such mammary matters, anthropologists do tend to agree that there are several styles of breasts among human females, and that these are related to racial, climactic and cultural factors. The beauty of Balinese breasts is renowned (they are what Ms. Reidman would call conic), while elongated breasts are typical of many African tribes.

Anthropologist Max Bartels has suggested 48 types of breasts, depending on whether they are (1) highly developed and exuberant, (2) full, (3) moderate or (4) small or flat; and, within each of these categories, whether they are (a) firm, (b) soft or (c) flabby; and, then, whether they are (I) bowl-shaped, (II) hemispherical, (III) conical or (IV) elongated. Systems have even been proposed to classify the areolae around the nipples into such groups as (1) cup-shaped, (2) hemispherical, (3) almost spherical, (4) disc-shaped. What is wrong with all these scientific categories is that they evade the classifications that are of real interest to lovers, husbands and infants, namely taste, responsivity, warmth, charge and excitability. We do not possess words for such concepts because it is still considered bad taste to even talk about them.

Thus, those women of Ra'ivavae are no more confused than the rest of humanity. Try to think logically about the question, should the breasts—or any other part of the body—be covered or uncovered. If you are at all typical, the results of your reflection will merely mirror your own ambivalences and perplexities. The case for nudism has been excellently presented by various spokesmen in the last century, but they have made few converts. Dr. Flugel's standard reference, *The Psychology of Clothes*, lists a variety of motives for covering the body—including protection from the elements, magic, and ritual uses, social-class identification, etc.—but notes that most of our designs and fashions seem diabolically designed to frustrate these motives, as if we have other purposes entirely. The two "other purposes" that Flugel especially stresses: modesty or shame—the desire to hide, on one hand—and decoration, or narcissism—the desire to be stared at—directly contradict each other. No wonder women's fashions are an object of such incessant and nervous humor; they are a manifestation of unconscious drives which most of us, male and female, would prefer to *keep* unconscious. Dr. Flugel, like Professor Knight Dunlop in the equally scholarly monograph, *The Development and Function of Clothing*, comes to the conclusion that if we were really sane we would go bare, like other animals. In all probability, our covering-up will be the first thing interplanetary visitors will notice about us, and it will give them the entire clue to our social lunacy.

Consider Arthur Schnitzler's once-sensational novel, *Fraulein Else*. The heroine, a proper young German lady, is put in a position where the only way to save her beloved father from bankruptcy is to submit to the desires of the villain. He, in turn, is more a voyeur than an activist and asks only to see her body nude. After the contract is signed and her father saved from the poorhouse, Fraulein Else gratifies, and frustrates, the villain by disrobing before him— and everybody else—in the lobby of a huge hotel. (She then commits suicide.) This plot electrified our grandparents because it almost makes explicit the unconscious function of clothing as creating a mystery which is to be revealed only to one person at time. Visitors to nudist camps are similarly frustrated when they realize that disrobing before a group has none of the "magic" of disrobing before a chosen individual.

A similar indication of the irrationality of our clothing mystique is the loud warning that civilization is imperiled whenever fashion changes too abruptly, especially if the change makes more flesh visible. In 1930, for instance, the earthquakes which shook Italy were attributed, by prominent Roman Catholic bishops, to the gowns recently imported from Paris. According to Dr. Flugel, one Romish divine even declared that Naples had been spared from the quakes because the Neopolitans "had resisted the present scandalous female fashions." The Vatican was notably less sensitive to the moral and meteorological implications of the murders and tortures practiced by Mussolini's government at that time, and nobody suggested that the labor union leaders left in an alley with bullets in their heads would provoke the Almighty to further tremors of the earth's crust.

Relatively sane people—who are still quite plentiful, although of course always a minority—seldom challenge the prevailing lunacy, knowing full well that path leads to the jailhouse or worse. In the country of the blind, after the one-eyed man has been executed, the two-eyed quickly learn to appease the blind and lunatic majority.

Do we exaggerate? Cousins, chew hard on this next bit: Donald Marshall's book *Ra'ivavae* points out that these modest women are part of a culture in which the primordial word for a supernatural power, *tiki*, mistranslated as "God" with a capital G by Thor Heyerdahl, also appears in the words *tikiroa*, the penis (literally: the long progenitor) and *tikipoto*, the clitoris (literally: the short progenitor); where the *tutiki*, or temple doorway, is described by a native informant as "the two thighs of the Earth Mother"; where religious ceremonies traditionally ended, just like the rites of the great mother in prehistoric Europe and Asia, with the priests and priestesses copulating and then rubbing the sperm on their heads for good *mana* (luck, energy, blessing). Yet, when the European doctor comes by, they cover their breasts—just as the village drunk telling a risqué joke to his cronies will lower his voice suddenly when the Reverend Snoot passes on the street. Yes, and just as an actress like Lana Turner, despite her well-publicized amours, was compelled for decades to speak dialogue on the screen implying that neither she nor the other actors nor the writer nor anyone in the world had ever doubted the sexual teachings of Francis Cardinal Spellman; just as psychologists as radical as Drs. Phillis and Eberhard Kronhausen, as recently as 1951, took all the "fucks"

out of a book on pornography and prudently substituted the
parenthetical "(vernacular for intercourse.)" A cynic might say
that we have never outgrown the primitive trait of worship-
ing the tribal madmen; and it is hard to say where humoring
their fantasies leaves off and sharing those fantasies begins.

(Ever hear of Emperor Norton? Joshua Norton, an English immigrant, failed as a businessman in San Francisco
during the 1850s. In 1861 he returned with an old army
uniform and a top hat, proclaimed himself emperor of the
United States and protector of Mexico, and began issuing his
own currency. Being then as now a whimsical town, San
Francisco humored him; restaurant owners not only accepted his strange-looking money, but competed with each
other for his patronage—especially after he became a tourist
attraction. Eventually, the newspapers were printing his
state proclamations and his absurd open letters to person-
ages such as Abraham Lincoln or Queen Victoria. The climax
of this career, in a sense, came one night when the vigilantes
decided to burn down Chinatown: The emperor stood before
them in the street, lowered his head and silently began
praying. The joke had become serious: The vigilantes dis-
persed and the Chinese were spared. When Norton the First
died in 1883, he had become so beloved that 30,000 people
turned out for his funeral. He is already elevated to saint-
hood in the *Principia Discordia*, quoted earlier, and perhaps
in another hundred years saying that he really acted like a
nut much of the time will get you a jail sentence. . . .)

O my brothers, rays or no rays, auras or no auras,
there's something spooky about the breasts that seven and
seventy taboos should be laid upon them. And if the attitudes of a Francis Cardinal Spellman seem strange to us,
we can get a real jolt and a further awareness of the spook-
specter-psycho wavelength by recalling Jack the Ripper's
famous note to Scotland Yard, which came in a box with a
breast amputated from his latest victim: "Hope you like this,"
Jack wrote in his cheerful way, "I ate the other one. . . ." Old

Leather Apron, as the whores called him, always performed what the press of the day evasively called "unspeakable mutilations" on the women he killed. It is, of course, only a coincidence that of all famous murderers (outside politics) his is the name best known to everybody. To say, as some Freudians do, that Jack's oral sadism (and peculiar sense of humor) is an expression of the frustrations all men feel in this civilization is sick, vile, un-American—the kind of thing only a Freudian can believe. Let us rush at once to the most anti-Freudian people around, the women's liberationists; in the February 1973 issue of *MS.* there was an article about the things men *must* realize and face up to by a man named Warren Farrell. Here's the place where you better start facing yourself, according to Mr. Farrell:

> My first views of women. Views as a sex object, learning to be "superior," developing contempt for women.

This is the sort of thing the editors at *MS.* really dig. They *know* that all men view women as objects, feel superior to them and regard them with contempt. Any suggestion that this might contain a bit of projection on their part is immediately rejected with the non-Aristotelian logic that *projection* is a Freudian discovery and Freud was a male chauvinist pig.

Well, I am not going to argue that there aren't any men who *do* regard women with contempt. There are quite a few who do, and in my experience it is possible, by gauging the extent of that contempt, to predict fairly accurately how long they were educated in conventional religious doctrines as children. It was not any libertine or libertarian sexual revolutionary of the sort *MS.* hates who said that women are "sacks of dung"; it was the Christian theologian Origen. It wasn't Freud or Kinsey or any "male scientist" (by definition inferior to female scientists) who said, "Every woman should be overwhelmed with shame at the very thought that she is a woman"; it was St. Clement of Alexandria. It wasn't from

Charles or Wilhelm Reich or Consciousness III that we received the noble affirmation, "Man, but not woman, is made
in the image of God. It is plain from this that women should
be subject to their husbands, and should be as slaves"; this
is from Gratian, the greatest authority on Catholic canon law
in the 13th Century. None of these men were sensualists or
functioning heterosexuals; they were all celibates, as was
Saint Thomas Aquinas, who wrote, "Woman is in subjection
because of the laws of nature. . . . Woman is subject to man
because of the weakness of her mind as well as of her body."

Now, I don't know who's a fool and who's wise, but
these men emphatically did not see the same breasts that I
see. They certainly were not "sexist," whatever that means;
they were quite clearly antisexist. They despised women
precisely because, as Saint Augustine made abundantly clear,
women caused them to have *feelings* (sexual and otherwise),
and they were determined to eliminate feelings and govern
themselves entirely by willpower. I'm not sure that they all
hoped to be able to wiggle their ears and break wind musi-
cally, as Augustine thought Adam did, but they wanted to
drive the servo-mechanisms (Fuller's "Phantom Captain")
out of the body and become entire monarchs of the flesh.
Now, this is impossible; the nervous system has been shaped
by evolution to be partly autonomic (involuntary) and only
partly under the voluntary control of the brain. The Church
Fathers were facing a biological brick wall and trying to *will*
themselves through to the other side. No wonder they sound
a little bit hysterical.

The normal male, on the other hand, the one who
doesn't share the Church Fathers' aversion to women and
women's bodies, has no contempt for the female *except and
to the extent that his early education came under the influence of
this antisexual teaching*. In fact, the chief characteristic of
normal men in our culture is not *contempt* for women but
ambiguity: An attempt to find some compromise between
their natural fondness for the other half of humanity and the

paranoid attitudes acquired from religious training. There is no evidence in biology or anthropology that the fondness is a hypocrisy or social pretense; it appears in animals far down the scale of evolution and, in one form or another, in virtually every human culture. It is part of being a male mammal. The aversion to women, however, is a late product existing only in certain religions which have split the nervous system schizophrenically in two and worship the "higher" (cortically controlled) aspect while dreading the old autonomic, self-regulating cybernetic function as "lower." Caught in this trap, some men have paranoid hallucinations about women, just as the starving have paranoid hallucinations about food, or the infant on schedule feeding probably had paranoid hallucinations about breasts.

The cynical folk-saying among men, "You can't live *with* women and you can't live *without* them," is a compromise between Christian misogyny and the biological needs of males. It would be much more true to say that you've got to either love them or hate them—to be truly indifferent is just about impossible. For good evolutionary reasons a man is aware of women in a quite different way than he is aware of tea kettles or umbrellas or even changes in the weather. This awareness effects him on all levels of his being, whether he is conscious of it or not. For example, an experiment you might enjoy trying some time—

Get a tape recorder, a newspaper, a good-looking young lady (who is hidden at first) and a male friend. Tell him you are conducting an experiment, but do not reveal the details. He is to read the newspaper aloud while you tape his voice; the young lady is, at this point, still not visible. After a few minutes, have her enter the room. Tell her to wait, and ask him to continue reading for a few minutes more. The results are quite amusing, and you will hear the difference right away, although he will not. Later, you can play the tape back and let him hear the difference also. What happens is that the moment an attractive female is in the room, his voice distinctly deepens and becomes even more obviously "masculine," and this happens without his consciously intending it. In most cases, he will be quite surprised, somewhat embarrassed and very intrigued at the difference.

This difference is called "sexism" by the women's liberationists and compared by them to "racism." After all, they say, to change your mental set when a Black man enters the room is obviously, undeniably, a form of racism, conscious or unconscious. Therefore, to change when a woman comes into the room is also a form of discrimination—*ergo*, "sexism."

This argument is plausible and a great many radical or liberal males, impressed by it, are trying to remove "sexism" from their personalities. The underground press and the women's lib periodicals of the 1970s were full of guilt-ridden confessionals by these chaps, telling how hard they had tried, admitting that they are still somewhat "sexist" and begging somebody to forgive them. *Liberals and radicals are particularly susceptible to guilt and always looking for forgiveness (they are almost all oral personalities, just as conservatives are usually anal personalities)*, and it might be amusing for some wretched hoaxer to convince them that the phototropic eye reflex (which causes the pupil to dilate when you walk from a lighted room to a dark one) is also shameful and perverted and should be eliminated. Within a few months, their periodicals would be full of shame-faced accounts of their attempts to conquer "implicit voyeurism" (as this reflex might be called) and pleas for somebody, somewhere, to forgive them for their lack of success.

Let us be perfectly clear here. "I have said what I have said; I have not said what I have not said," as Count Korzybski, the semanticist, used to tell pupils who misconstrued him. Economic discriminations against women is profitable, just as economic discrimination against Blacks is profitable. Both will continue as long as they are profitable. Both will decrease toward zero in proportion to the extent that women and Blacks organize to fight for their rights and make such discrimination unprofitable—just as exploitation of labor has decreased in exact proportion to the extent that labor unions have become powers to be reckoned with.

Discrimination, then, is not a sexual issue at all. White Americans have no special or innate sexual interest in Blacks or Mexican-Americans or Indians, but they have nevertheless exploited these groups economically whenever it was profitable. Men without any sex drive (i.e. eunuchs) could exploit women on the labor market just as thoroughly as normal men have. The attempt to trace female oppression back to the sex drive and the weird notion that getting rid of the sex drive would automatically abolish this exploitation is a folly comparable to claiming that if employers gave up some other great delight of their private lives (art, sports, hobbies or whatever) they would then pay better wages.

No: The attack on "sexism" has nothing to do with any legitimate economic aspiration of women as a group; it is, rather, a stalking horse behind which certain impassioned spokeswomen are releasing their long-pent-up reactive hostility toward men.

What does happen when sex is banished from the human organism, to the extent that this is possible at all? Freud's examination of the various neuroses, psychoses, hysterias, psychosomatic illnesses, etc., is only a partial answer. The full story is seemingly much uglier. The dwindling and sprouting forth again of the breast between 1920 and 1945 is something that needs to be seen in a much larger context. For instance: The classical Romans had a curious custom of measuring the breasts of a bride just before the wedding and then again on the morning after the marriage was consummated. Any increase in size was taken as evidence that she had been a virgin, because "everybody knew" that the beginning of a regular sex life caused the breasts to swell. A really notable increase was a sign of special vigor and virility on the part of the groom.

Was this entirely superstition? We have already pointed

out the existence of what Dr. Alex Comfort calls a "hot line" between the breasts and genitalia—a feedback loop which causes sexual caresses at either end of the circuit to produce symptoms of excitation at the other hand. Excite the clitoris and the nipples harden; suck the nipples and the vagina becomes moist. (This even helps the vagina return to natural size after childbirth, if the woman breast-feeds the newborn instead of plasticizing it with a bottle.) But the body is even more amazing then this, and responds to ideas, sometimes, as if it were made of silly-putty. Witness the well-recorded cases of hysterical pregnancy, in which a sexually repressed woman imagines she has been raped and then produces quite convincing abdominal swellings and even stops menstruating. Cases of hysterical blindness, deafness, paralysis and endless "psychogenic" illnesses are also well-documented. How much did the Roman superstition cause the breasts of well-satisfied brides to swell in actuality (thereby continuing the "superstition")? How much of the vanished breast of the 1920s was arranged outside the body by special bras and clothing—and how much went on inside through self-repression? We can hardly begin to guess.

Some remnant of the Roman superstition seems to linger on in the widespread male idea that large-breasted women *must* be more promiscuous than average. There is an element of self-debasing wish-fulfillment in this, since behind it is the unspoken notion, "If she'll sleep with *anyone*, maybe I've got a chance." Women's lib writers, who have caught the wish-fulfillment here, seem to have missed the intense self-doubt also involved. On the reverse side, some large-breasted women cash in on the social myth by entering show business and becoming (as the jargon has it) sex objects; but many others become extremely shy and much more self-conscious than women with average-size mammaries. For every Jayne Mansfield sporting about in a tight dress, there is a similarly stacked woman waiting for a bus on a street corner, disguising this attribute with a loose inside sweater

covered by a second sweater with buttons half-open creating
a look of amorphous mystery.

The direct contradiction of the Roman belief—evidently
influenced by the Christian bias that sex couldn't possibly
make anything better—was expressed by Dr. Theodore Bell
in 1821 in a book entitled *Kalogynomia* (roughly, "The Book
of Female Beauty"). Large and rounded breasts (the sign of
sexual experience, according to the Romans) actually signi-
fied virginity, Dr. Bell claimed. On the other hand, women
of experience had breasts which sagged or showed "irregular-
ity." The wise man, he added, would choose the first type
for a wife, presumably to have the delight of causing the first
sag to appear. I frankly prefer the Roman superstition, if one
must choose between idiocies. A famous verse by Catullus
— *Non illam nutrux, oriente luce revisens hesterno collum poteret
circumdare filo*[29] — at least makes it sound like a happy
accomplishment.

Dr. Bell's notions are an aspect of the great 19th-
Century trend to find "scientific" proofs of Christian dogmas—
especially, to show that every act considered sinful by the
church fathers was, in some way or other, harmful to health.
A general impression was created, aided by all the best
medical men of the time, that sexual sins in particular left
horrible effects on the body and marked the face with a clear
expression of "evil." The last product of this hysteria, turning
it into art, was Oscar Wilde's *The Picture of Dorian Gray*, in
which the hero evades this great Victorian nemesis by trans-
ferring the disfigurements to his portrait. He leads a high
and glorious life of vice, but forever looks young and innocent, while the painting magically turns into a monster
suitable for Hollywood's horror movies, where in fact it has
already landed twice. (The fact that Wilde was writing about
homosexuality in code added to the shock effect of this fable;
and, in all three of his trials, counsel attempted constantly,
by the baiting techniques permissible in cross-examination,
to trip him into admitting this. He denied everything with a

straight face, but went to jail anyway.)

Naturally, the Victorian attitude, like the Roman, tends to become a self-fulfilling prophecy to some extent. An old Chinese parable tells of a farmer who found some cash missing and became convinced that a neighbor's son had taken it. Sure enough, every time he looked at the boy thereafter, a flush of shame and a furtive look in the eyes revealed the consciousness of guilt. Then, surprisingly, the farmer found the money where he had misplaced it. The next day he saw the boy again and a more fair-faced and open-eyed lad you'd never hope to meet. This tale, of course, is a warning against what Freud later called *projection* and Buddha called *maya*—seeing your own fantasies wherever you look; but it also illustrates the way people respond to social expectations. The boy was self-conscious because he sensed that he was being stared at in a hostile and suspicious manner.

The Romans and Dr. Bell had one thing in common; they passively watched and waited to see what nature would do to the breasts. Many peoples have been more activist, as indicated by the uplift bra—which goes back, in one form or another, over 2000 years. Other folk have taken even stronger action to obtain the right kind of look. For instance, in New Guinea, young girls attempt to force the breasts to grow large and round by such methods as these, quoted in Ploss's *Femina Libido Sexualis*:

> A number of ants of two special kinds are collected; their heads are pulled off and they are rubbed on the breasts. The sharp liquid stings the skin, causing slight swelling which is increased by dabbing with nettles. The method is naturally not efficacious at first but must be repeated. The Papuans, however, are of the opinion that it makes the breasts grow more quickly; and if the girl endures and perseveres good results will not fail to follow. But this cure must not be applied while the girl is facing the sea, for the waves that wash the shore would otherwise . . . wash away her slowly expanding breasts.

On the other hand, several African tribes, in which the low-slung or "droopy" look is preferred, tie the breasts down with bands of twine to prevent the upright look the Papuans (and most Americans today) treasure. The more one plunges into anthropological studies, on the breasts or on any human passion, the more inclined one is to pronounce that all men and women are mad. How about this one, if you happen to believe that we are reasoning animals? In Spain, during the 16th and 17th Centuries, the women covered their breasts with lead plates, creating a deliberate concave in place of the natural convexity. Further: The Amazons (who may have been historical) amputated one breast, while mutilations have been practiced in Africa, Oceana, the Americas and among the Skopsi sect in Russia.

The human brain is in many ways like the parrot brain: it will repeat anything it hears. Its celebrated rationality seldom helps much, for it will understand and believe what it is repeating, unlike the parrot, and few at any time are resolute enough to doubt what everybody else is saying in the entire tribe. If big breasts are locally beautiful, women will torture themselves to get big breasts; if little breasts are the local fad, again no pain is too great to achieve that goal. (Anybody who thinks this is a quality only of the female mind should read some of the criticisms of circumcision by doctors who oppose the practice and ask why we continue to inflict this on male infants.) Everywhere, at all times, folks can see the looniness of the next tribe down the road, but nobody can ever see the lunacy of his or her own tribe.

Quite similarly, if society expects large-breasted women to be virginal, quite a few of them will follow that program; and if society expects large-breasted women to be promiscuous, a certain number of them will adopt that life-script. But more: the body, as much as the mind, can be shaped by these social definitions, and a young girl may develop large breasts and a promiscuous life-style *together* in joint response to some strong social force telling her that's the kind of girl she is. At least, increasing numbers of psychologists are beginning to believe this. While some biologists are still debating the old *nature* versus *nurture* controversy—whether we are primarily the result of inborn gene patterns or of subsequent nourishment after birth—and others accept the synthetic view that we are a combination of both (which certainly sounds more reasonable on the face of it), recent evidence indicates that we are actually the product of three variables: nature, nurture and mind.

According to a show-biz legend, a young actress trained in the Stanislavski method was hired for a bit part in a Marx Brothers' movie. "Now, in this scene," the director explained to her, "you come on in a bathing suit. Harpo sees you, honks his horn and lunges. You run off screaming. Got it?" She nodded thoughtfully. "What's my motivation?" she asked.

This is not as absurd as it seems. The body responds to a mental set instantly in many subtle ways that communicate at once to every observer, even though this message is nonverbal. The Stanislavski training, with its emphasis on permeating the whole body with the personality of the character being portrayed, is quite similar in many ways to certain devices of Reichian, Perlsian, Lowenite and other modern psychotherapeutic techniques. Reich taught young psychiatrists who studied with him to observe every characteristic movement and posture of the patient and *imitate* them, saying that in this way one would begin to feel what the patient feels. Similarly, a Stanislavski actor may end up decreasing the height of his neck by two inches as he gradually "feels his way into" the character of a timid person. Rod Steiger, in particular, has a marvelous capacity to seemingly shrink or grow depending on what sort of person he is playing.

Similar "Stanislavski exercises" *performed in dead earnest and not as play-acting* by desperate infants, children and adolescents trying to become what society around them says they should be almost certainly have some influence on the body type they eventually develop. Such at least is the hypothesis of researchers as divergent as Franz Alexander, Wilhelm Reich, Alexander Lowen, Frederick Perls, William Schutz, Ashley Montague and dozens of others. Thus, with all due acknowledgment to nature and nurture, *some* men are burly and tough-looking because they've been trying all their lives to be human tanks or battering rams; *some* timid souls are short and skinny because they're constantly engaged in giving the impression "Pay no attention, I'm too small and insignificant to bother you"; and, almost certainly, *some* sagging breasts indicate profound defeatism about life and sex, while *some* high, pointed breasts indicate a spirit of adventure and eagerness.

The "catty" remark, "She's not as pretty as she looks," said by one envious female of another, is not as illogical as it seems. It means that the woman in question, with all the willpower in the world, has not quite compensated for mediocre nature and nurture, but has compensated well enough that it requires really close looking to *see* that she's really fairly ordinary. Nor is this entirely a matter of makeup, clothing and other artificial or external beauty aids. The spark of life—whether we call it the soul or the libido or the bioenergy or the kundalini or whatnot—is either burning bright or flickering dismally; and this feeling-tone is expressed in every muscle, every gland, every tint of color on the skin.

Contrary to one of Hollywood's best-loved myths, the prettiest girls are usually the brightest ones, and the dull ones are usually dull all the way through, mentally and physically. This has been confirmed in test after test, even in studies performed by skeptical psychologists who suspected that teachers are unconsciously prejudiced in favor of nice-looking children. No: Even when we use I.Q. scales graded by persons who haven't seen the subjects, handsome boys and pretty girls almost always score higher than average. (Jayne Mansfield, almost always cast as the stereotyped "dumb blonde" by Hollywood, actually graduated with honors from a reputable university.)

In the typical Hollywood college movie, the good-looking hero and heroine are dull-normal in intelligence, while their humorously presented "best friends" (or stooges), the homely guy and the ugly girl, are the class geniuses. In real life, it is usually the other way around. As Eric Berne has pointed out over and over, when people find a game-strategy that seems to work, they play it all the time in everything they do; and for some this consists of winning-by-winning and for others it is winning-by-losing. This is generally true of animals, also (except for the collie dog, which was deliberately bred for a long nose by several generations of misguided breeders until, as some wit said, the head got so long that the brains were pushed out through the ears). Otherwise the famous signs of "bright eyes and bushy tails" almost always indicate a bright, curious nature and a warm personality in a handsome body.

It could hardly be otherwise. The basic processes of neurology are excitation (abbreviated + in the textbooks) and inhibition (abbreviated −). As Wilhelm Reich said, with perhaps some exaggeration, you are either growing (+) or shrinking (−), either advancing toward your goals or retreating from them; it is the same energy in all cases, either flowing freely and felt as excitation and health, or blocked (*Besetzung*, cathexis, "being stuck") and felt as inhibition and anxiety.

A rival school of depth psychology gives a different, but equally illuminating, view of what it means to stifle part of the organism.

According to Carl Gustav Jung's theory of the collective unconscious, certain archetypes or numinous symbols recur spontaneously in all peoples everywhere. These images preceded the invention of language, Jung claims, and are born with us just like our hair color, our race or the rest of our genetic endowment. As Joseph Campbell points out in *The*

Masks of God, this seemingly extravagant theory has much to support it in ethological research. Chickens, for instance, have an inborn hawk-image in their tiny brains: They will not only flee from a actual hawk but from a cardboard outline of a hawk if it is floated above them in the air. Any skeptical argument that the chickens' unconditioned fear of hawks is caused by the smell of the hawk collapses in the face of this experiment: It is the shape—a shape the newborn chick has never seen—which immediately triggers the fear-response.

If we have similar archetypes (as Jung called them), it is no metaphor to speak of Marilyn Monroe or Raquel Welch as sex goddesses. These actresses, by careful and intuitive study, have incorporated and projected the archetype and serve, for us, the same role that Ishtar served for the Babylonians, Aphrodite for the Greeks, Venus for the Romans, etc.

Then, too, the other aspect of the goddess, the all-giving mother whom I have already categorized as an extension of the infant's fantasies at the breast, is also still alive, even in an officially Christian and patriarchal culture. For instance, Emma Lazarus projected this image onto the Statue of Liberty in a famous poem. The poem struck the same archetypal level in the mass psyche, and the key lines were then inscribed on the statue itself. (You'll find them on the book held in her lift hand.) These lines are as direct an expression of the all-providing mother as the witch-queen's speech quoted earlier:

> Give me your tired, your poor, your huddled masses
> Yearning to breathe free,
> The wretched refuse of your teeming shore.
> Send these, tempest-tossed, to me:
> I lift my lamp beside the golden Door

(American culture was too anal to live up to this totally oral fantasy, so the last line should now read "And I'll send them right back where they came from.")

According to Jung, the archetypes wax and wane just

like living organisms or species. Thus, at one time society will be obsessed with the mother goddess, at another time with the younger sex goddess, then again with the father god and at another date with the suffering young hero who dies and rises again (Osiris, Tammuz, Baldur, Adonis, Christ, etc.). The more tolerant or psychologically acute civilizations have deified all of these—usually together with a trickster god (Loki, Set, the American Indians' Coyote, Satan, the joker aspect of Krishna, etc.)—and allowed each person to choose one in-particular as personal deity, or to switch from one to another at different stages of life. The intolerant patriarchal religions of Judaism, Christianity and Islam have taken the opposite path, enforced one Father God on everybody and condemned all comparison shopping—the Old Testament calls it "whoring after strange gods"—as the most wretched of all sins.

But, O my brothers, remember what Dr. La Barre the anthropologist said back on page 28 about the origin of the gods in the nuclear human family: There is no way of activating an archetype (in Jung's terms) without starting the process that activates the others. The mother was pushed into the background by Christianity for ten centuries, but then she surged forward again and in Latin countries you will see her image more often than the Father and the Son together. The Trickster had his own cult in the Middle Ages and still does in Anton Szandor Lavey's First Church of Satan in San Francisco. And the sex goddess reappears not only in movies but in novels and paintings. Which old master, however devoutly Christian, has not left us at least one glorious Venus?

So, too, the body parts—*chakras*, the Hindus call them—are each associated with an archetype. The pineal chakra, or "third eye" in the forehead, is always associated with the most destructive aspect of the father god in the West or with the image of Shiva the Destroyer in the East (but this is also positive, since the highest mystic trance is destructive in the sense of exploding the rational ego and allowing the other body centers to come alive and "speak"). The mother goddess and sex goddess are centered in the breast and genitals respectively (but each overlaps the other to some extent, so that the mother goddess is chiefly in the breast and the sex goddess chiefly in the genitals, but each is also at times in the other area).

We still think of love in the language of this ancient symbolism (which underlies kundalini yoga, sexual occultism and the Chinese acupuncture healing methods). The seat of love is in the breasts and usually symbolized in art by a "valentine" heart—a conventional shape which does not resemble the real heart very much. It actually looks like a simplified form of the old religious emblems of the female genital to be found in any book on the mother religions. We use this very sexy heart on valentine cards, where it is usually shown pierced by a phallic arrow, and it always appears in Roman Catholic art, surmounted by a cross— which was, of course, a phallic image in Egypt millennia before Christ. (The cross "seems to be based on some part of the human body," Budge comments with an owlish solemnity in his *Amulets and Talismans*. Knight and Wright in *Sexual Symbolism* leave no doubt that the original religious crosses symbolized exactly what they look like. The Jehovah's Witnesses do not use crosses because Charles Russell, their founder, glanced into a few texts on the matriarchal fertility-religions, found out what the cross really was, and recoiled in Victorian horror.)

This valentine heart, with or without cross and arrow, is a very pervasive and resonant symbol. Even in a culture as far removed from Western traditions as China, the symbol for human emotion included the glyph for the heart (along with the liver, curiously). Expressions such as "I felt as if my heart would break" or "I felt as if my heart would burst with joy" are known to be medically inaccurate, but if we take the valentine heart as a symbol not of the heart itself but of the heart chakra which corresponds to a nerve cluster governing both the actual heart (and blood circulation) and the lungs (and respiration), these expressions seem to contain much truth. The yogis who specialize in kundalini yoga confirmed this with successful results for a few thousand years (as have the Chinese acupuncturists). So, too, has there been growing confirmation from those Western psychiatrists and psychologists who have taken a body-centered approach to therapy. This includes the Reichian "orgonomists," the Perlsian "gestaltists," the Lowenian "bio-energeticists," and the Rolfian "Rolfers" (as they are actually called); in addition, those working with Alexander's relaxation techniques and Charlotte Selver's "sensory awareness" have reported similar results—as have countless LSD trippers. Whether the chakras actually are "points of contact between the body and the Astral Realm," as the Hindus believe, is open to question: but the evidence clearly indicates that they are neural centers where emotions can effect the body for years after the emotional experience itself, and where, conversely, bodily manipulations can ease or even cure stubborn emotional problems.

A person who says his heart is leaping with joy or breaking with sorrow is not talking nonsense, even if the actual heart is only secondarily involved. It is his fourth chakra, connected with both heart and lungs, that is expanding with joyous energy or contracting with despair. In the latter case, if the sorrow last too long or is too unbearable, physical problems will eventually appear, sometimes actually involving a heart attack. (Bruno Klopfer, M.D., has even collected statistics showing that in a group of randomly chosen cancer patients, the majority had some major bereavement or prolonged depression within a period of six months before the cancer symptoms appeared.)

William C. Shutz suggests, in this connection, that men with especially small penises probably had very repressive childhoods and built up muscular armors around the groin area in order to numb the "sinful" feelings there; these armors cut down on the oxygen and blood supply and thus atrophied the growth of the organ. Similarly, Franz Alexander, M.D., testing a group of women with cancer of the cervix, found a previous history of frigidity in most of them, while—more to our purpose—in women with cancer of the breast he found a background of emotional conflict with the mother. The denial of the breast by the women's fashions of the 1920s, and the denial of the function of the breast by the simultaneous fad of bottle-feeding, obviously represent such a surrender motivated by emotional problems in fourth ("heart") chakra, shared by the archetypal goddesses of mothering and sex.

The rise and fall of the neckline throughout history, if this analysis is correct, should correspond with the rise and fall of the goddesses in the human psyche. Looking to the ancient world we see at once that in Crete, where the mother goddess was supreme, the women did not cover their breasts at all. Surviving art works strongly suggest that the rib-cage girdle was reinforced so as to push the breasts upward in the manner of a modern "uplift" bra but without actually covering them. Nearby, the Babylonian religion contained an element of sex worship institutionalized as hierogamy: The highest temple contained in its highest room a couch on which a priestess copulated with a god. (Probably—so one suspects from Frazer's *Golden Bough*—the god appeared as a mortal man, a wandering stranger, and was recognized as a divinity by some special sign. The ancient Scythians, for instance, recognized disguised gods by the red hair on them—but, alas, in that case they were not expected to fornicate with a priestess but instead were torn to pieces and scattered over the fields to make the crops grow better[30].)

In Greece, the Athenians became the most notable male chauvinists in the ancient world. Their women were required to keep their breast covered from earliest times. Later, the robe was compulsorily lengthened from the cute mini-skirt still seen in some early statues to floor-length costume that covered the legs thoroughly. All political liberties possessed by women elsewhere in Greece (e.g., the right to own personal property) were taken away from the ladies of Athens—in short, they were reduced to the state which in our society is considered normal. As a crowning ignominy, they were forbidden to leave their homes unless accompanied by their fathers or, later, by their husbands. The "mythological" explanation for all this patriarchal fascism was that Athens had once been attacked by a tribe of Amazons—warrior women who amputated one breast, killed all male infants and had a permanent grudge against men—after which the Athenian men were somewhat paranoid about their own women. Curiously, this mythological explanation may have considerable truth in it, for Russian archaeologists have recently found remnants of an Amazon society in southern Russia, just where the Athenian legends claim the original Amazons came from.

In Rome, a husband had the legal right to kill his wife if she got on his nerves, *and he could not be held accountable for this in any court of law.* (Roman men had the same right to kill female, or male, slaves.) It is not surprising that the goddesses survived in only an attenuated form in Athens and Rome and were put in a distinctly inferior position to the father gods, Zeus and Jupiter—at least in the official state religion. Where the rites of the goddess survived at all they were the target of furious satire by patriarchal intellectuals like Juvenal, who says in his *Sixth Satire*:

> The secret rites of the Good Goddess
>   are pretty well known
> When a flute stirs their loins and
>   the Maenids of Priapus groan
> And howl in frenzy form music and
>   wine and toss their hair.
> Oh, how they burn for intercourse,
>   what cries declare

Their throbbing lust, how wet their
  legs with streaming juices . . .

They're females without veneer and
  around the ritual den
Rings a cry from every corner: "We're
  ready! Bring in the men!"
And if the stud is sleeping, the
  young man's ordered to wrap
Himself in a robe and hurry over.
  If he's not on tap
A raid is made on the slaves; remove
  the hope of a slave,
They'll hire a water carrier. If
  they can't find a man, to save
The day they'll get a donkey to
  straddle their itchy behinds.
Oh, would that our ancient rites
  at least in public shrines
Were purged of these filthy acts[31]!

You will find the same tone (and some of the details) in
the writing of Christian Inquisitors about the witches' Sab-
bath 14 or 15 centuries later. Most of it, of course—like *Zap
Comix* portraying a women's liberation meeting—is the fe-
vered imagination of Juvenal himself, who probably knew
only that sex was *somehow* involved in the rites of the good
goddess(*bona dea*) and filled in the rest with what he *conjectured*
was typical female sexuality. The occult thrillers of Dennis
Wheatley are full of the same sort of nonsense; a certain
type of anal-patriarchal male mind can only conceive of
sexual ritual in terms of compulsive and hysterical "going
berserk" or swinelike "wallowing in filth." (These types never
realize that the filth is in their own semantic reflexes.) A man
with similar hangups about food might imagine that at the
Holy Communion in a Catholic church the maddened worshipers stuff themselves with the bread, roll on the floor and
knock each other about trying to get at the wine. Aleister

Crowley commented that Spiritualists and other holier-than-thou types were always asking him how they could attend a ritual orgy and he always answered, with literal truth, that he didn't know about such things; but he was the foremost sexual occultist of our century.

(The stupidity of the question prompted and necessitated the nature of the answer. It is, after all, like asking a prima ballerina if you could attend her next wrestling match.)

Sexual repression (together with the perversions that usually accompany it) was quick to follow the suppression of women in Rome. Ovid was sent into exile, apparently because his love lyrics were considered licentious by somebody in the palace (or else, as other authorities have guessed, because the Hindu-like outburst of vegetarianism and pacifism at the end of his *Metamorphoses* seemed subversive); but meanwhile emperors like Nero and Caligula and Commodus set records for sexual and other perversities that were not to be equaled until De Sade's equally astonishing but fictitious creations. If the popular cliché says that these sadists "had no heart," and if the history of Roman imperialism and exploitation of the world suggests that the whole governing class "had no heart," then we can say that in a Jungian sense **the decline of the mother goddess and the repression of the female had produced a deadening in the heart chakra, the seat of the loving and compassionate emotions.** A mystical-sounding notion, indeed, and I blush to offer it, but Ashley Montagu, physical anthropologist, has published statistics in his book *The Direction of Human Development* showing that children deprived of mothering are more likely to become criminals than others and are also more likely to develop psychoses. One of the most famous experiments in ethology demonstrated that monkeys deprived of normal nursing at the breast in infancy failed to develop a normal sex drive in adulthood. Psychiatrist Joe K. Adams has reported a study in which rats, deprived of oral sex play, lost all interest in copulation and began cannibalistically devouring each other.

Gershon Legman's Simple Simon slogan "Make Love, Not War" has an element of real truth in it. When the former is blocked, the drive toward the latter does seem to increase.

It seems that when people "give up" or "give away" part of their bodies, in the sense of psychologists Perls and Schutz, they do this by repressing activity in the nerve cluster that makes up the appropriate chakra, and this is marked, in religious history, by the decline of the deity associated with that chakra. Conversely, reactivating a chakra brings the deity back into prominence. Thus, the rites which are based on concentrating the "mind" and/or the bioenergy in the genital chakra—such as Tantric yoga and the Western equivalents associated with the troubadours, Illuminati, "alchemists," etc.—reactivate the sex goddess, while anything which makes the breast or the act of breast-feeding more conspicuous tends to reactivate also the mother goddess.

Thus, as Charles Seltman points out in his classic study, *Women in Antiquity*, very early *terra cotta* figurines from the Near East show females offering their breasts either *to* or in imitation *of* the goddess. "They either hold or squeeze their breasts," Seltman explains, "or else they clasp their hands over the solar plexus beneath their breasts."[32] This tradition may have lasted long enough to be the inspiration of Eleanor of Aquitaine's flaunting of these emblems of the goddess in the homeland of the father gods Jehovah and Allah. This is not incredible, since many scholars accept Thomas Wright's suggestion, in his *Worship of the Generative Organs*, that the mysterious Baphomet worshiped by Eleanor's contemporaries, the Knights Templar, was actually *Pater Met'* or Father Mithra, the sun god of the Roman Legions. . . .

The Virgin Mary suddenly thereafter infiltrated herself to the very center of Catholic worship and, in Latin American countries, often seems to have displaced Father, Son and Holy Ghost rather thoroughly. Portraits of her nursing her Divine Son (strikingly similar to the similar ikons of Egyptian Isis which seem to have survived from a quai-matriarchal period) were executed by almost all the major artists of the next several centuries. This totally oral archetype almost became the central symbol of Christianity for a while (one can imagine how Augustine would have felt if he had returned), and there was only a slight hiatus of Mariolatry during the Reformation and Counter-Reformation. The Protestants frequently charged, quite accurately, that the whole Mary cult was unscriptural and a reversion to paganism, but this did not stop the slow steady progression of the archetype. Objectively, a humanitarian must consider the tendency good, since it has markedly decreased the old anal paranoia of the churchmen. Legends in which a dreadful sinner is saved from the wrath of God at the very last moment by Mary's compassion are known in every Catholic country and could have come from the cheerful Greeks or the sentimental Romans. Notably, the Protestant sects which have excluded Mary have kept the greatest intensity of the traditional Christian bigotry and intolerance. As William Carlos Williams emphasized in his *In the American Grain*, this is obvious the moment you cross the Rio Grande, for from that point southward to the bottom tip of South America the population is still largely Indian or part-Indian, whereas from that point north the Indians have virtually disappeared. This seems to be the difference between being conquered by half-matrist Catholics and being conquered by totally patrist Protestants. For a while in the 1960s, rumblings about "bombing them back to the Stone Age" suggested that the same genocidal policy was about to be repeated in Vietnam. It would be interesting to try to discover how many of the young women who bared their breasts in front of the Pentagon in October 1967 (as reported in Norman Mailer's *The Armies of the Night*) had any conscious idea of what they were doing, and how many were just activated, in Jung's terms, by the re-emergence of the archetype via the sweater girl of the 1940s, the Playmate of the 1950s and the unforgettable poster of the Vietnamese woman with a child at her breast used in all the peace marches of the 1960s. It does seem that in some sense the goddess has returned.

There is even a tendency to bring back the giant-breasted goddess image of the Stone Age; this can be seen not only in cartoons and the illustrations on adventure magazine covers but on many actual women. Some of this is nature, some is nurture, some is mind; but some is obviously silicone. In fact, the silicone injection treatment to build larger breasts is already fashionable enough to have started a debate in medical and women's lib circles comparable to that raging around the oral contraceptive. Naturally, doctors who make their living off this treatment are most painfully sincere in announcing its safety; while those not so intimately involved in the dollars-and-cents side of the matter are more inclined to worry about possible dangers. (Lord Macauley said a century ago that if there were a financial interest involved, the law of gravity would be thrown into dispute.)

The tendency of the human being to mutate, or to imagine that he or she is mutating, to fit a social ideal, has many strange consequences erotically. We have already seen that the penis and the breasts changed and enlarged as we evolved from apes with seasonal sexuality to humans with year-round sexuality; we have also seen the breast wax and wane in accord with society's fads. Wayland Young points out something that indicates either a mutation of the female torso or a mutation of the eye of the artist:

> We have seen how in Greece and Rome fucking was not held to be a special thing to which description and depiction were inapplicable. But in the Middle Ages the eye and ear of art were withdrawn from the meeting of man and woman. More; the eye was withdrawn from the bodies themselves of men and women, so that the Gothic nude was not a man or woman but a symbol of something else; of lust, perhaps, or wisdom, or folly, or plenty. All this is ably discussed in Sir Kenneth Clark's book, *The Nude*, where he puts the thing in geometrical terms. The distance between the breasts of a woman in Gothic

art is half that between breast and navel. In classical and
Renaissance art, the two breasts and the navel form an equilateral triangle and the distance between breast and navel is the
same as the distance between navel and crotch. . . . Now
anybody who has looked at a woman knows that the triangle
breast-breast-navel is about equilateral, and not elongated with
the apex downward. It can hardly be supposed that Western
woman mutated about the fourth century A.D. and mutated
back again about 1500, all of Western women together in one
move, so it must be that Medieval artists were not painting
and sculpting what they saw.[33]

Or was it? Judging by our experience in this century, after
that medieval anatomical ideal was formulated, a large number of women, by one means or another, made themselves
look like it, thereby perpetuating the ideal. Study our 1920s
illustrations and this science fiction hypothesis will seem not
entirely incredible.

Somebody once wrote a story illustrating the cultural
differences between the great nations of the modern world.
An international scientific body, in this yarn, offers an award
for the best scholarly study of the elephant. When the judges
have narrowed their choice down to seven outstanding en-
tries they see that the treatise from a French university *savant*
is entitled "Sexual Practices of Elephants," the English contri-
bution is "Scientific Design for Elephant-Hunting Guns," a
Spanish scholar has presented "Patterns of Challenge and
Honor Between Male Elephants," a Russian has offered "Exploitation of Elephants by the Monopolists of the Ivory
Industry," a German has brought forth "Introductory Study
of the Elephant's Toe-Nails" (4 volumes), a South African
(white, presumably) wrote "Keeping the Elephant in His
Proper Place" and an American composed "Breeding Bigger
and better Elephants."

The emphasis on sheer size in America is one of the first
things noted by foreign visitors. The Empire State Building
is so absurdly high that an airplane once collided with it.

Then the even-taller World Trade Center was built in New York. Tired of always being second to New York, Chicago constructed the latest "tallest building in the world"—the John Hancock Building—although a rational mind might suggest that Chicago is much more in need of housing for the poor, asphalt to plug up the moonlike craters in the sidewalks, gigantic fans to blow the air pollution back to the steel mills of Gary and a few other civilized amenities. Hollywood still advertises "a cast of thousands" on every epic, as if sheer numbers can compensate for lack of any other recommendation. Our politicians, especially our presidents, always emphasize the astronomical figures spent on government projects, apparently on the assumption that it distracts us from the glaring fact that few of these "wars" (on poverty, on drugs, on Asiatics, or whatnot) accomplish what they are set up to do. Even the reading public, those last few remnants of the pre-McLuhan age, shares this great American mystique, and publishers know that it is easier to sell a 1200-page tome for $30 than a 200-page novella for $10. *Bulk is best*, is our national motto. It is even possible that the Attila-the-Hun approach to Vietnam, in which our government dropped three times as many bombs as were used all over Europe and North Africa in World War II *to subdue a tiny country the size of New England* and thereby horrified most of the world and much of our own populace, was also based on the simple notion that "if it's bigger than before, it's better than before."

Even our gay citizens, whose spokesmen claim they are alienated from and (they are not above hinting) superior to our "straight culture," share this obsession with sheer dimension. The homosexual scrawls in lavatories always claim penile sizes suitable for *Guinness Book of World Records*—"I have nine inches and love sailors," "I have fourteen inches and dig the leather scene," etc. These are probably lies, unless a lot of queer horses have learned how to hold fountain pens in their hooves and scrawl on bathroom walls. (They are also often deceptive in other ways, according to a gay liberation writer I know. If you call the phone numbers given, you sometimes find yourself talking to the vice squad, college instructors who have made themselves unpopular with students, the John Birch Society or similarly unappetizing and unprepared gentry. Another friend, hetero, once called a "Rose" who claimed to give "the best blow-job in Brooklyn only $10" and found himself listening to a recording of a sweet old lady who reads Bible stories to children.)

The esteemed Mailer did not think to inform his readers about the size of the breasts bared at the Pentagon, but it is doubtful that there were any silicone jobs there. By and large, radical females tend to be naturalists, inclined to public breast-feeding, organic foods, natural childbirth, a preference for yoga or chiropractics rather than conventional medicine, and a deep Consciousness III aversion to anything "plastic." Nevertheless, they and the silicone-injected star of the go-go bar are both, in different ways, manifesting the reemergence of the goddess. The Pentagon, traditional shape inscribed inside a starlike pentagram in workings of Satanic magic seeking power to destroy and blight, is so apt a location for this demonstration of recrudescent matrist values that one could almost suspect the organizers of the protest had read Jung and were attempting to employ his psychological laws consciously.

In that case, the scrawls of "Pentagon Sucks" later found on the walls could almost be interpreted as an attempt to remind the Joint Chiefs of Staff of their own primordial mammalian nature.

---

[28] New York: Doubleday, 1961.

[29] By the light of dawn, the thread which yesterday encompassed her breasts no longer meets.

[30] Like most magic rituals, human sacrifice had a rationale when first invented. If the victim's body is scattered in the fields, the crops *will* grow better—not because of his "life force" necessarily (which is what the shaman thinks) but because of the *nitrogen* in the human body. The replacement of human sacrifice by animal sacrifice, which Frazer attrib-

utes to the growing moral sense of mankind, would not have succeeded if the magicians had not discovered that a dead animal gives as much to the soil as a dead human.

[31] *The Satires of Juvenal*, trans. by Hubert Creekmore (New York: New American Library, 1963).

[32] Charles Seltman, *Women in Antiquity* (London: Thames and Hudson, 1956).

[33] Wayland Young, *Eros Denied* (New York: Grove Press, 1964).

7. Making a clean breast of it

I remember [Marilyn Monroe] on the screen, huge as a colossus doll, mincing and whispering and simply hopping her way into total availability, total vulnerability. Watching her, I felt angry, even humiliated, but I didn't understand why. After all, Jane Russell was in the movie, too . . . so it wasn't just the vulnerability that all big-breasted women seem to share.

—Gloria Steinem[34]

This "vulnerability" of big-breasted women, we have tried to show, is the result of the peculiar hatred of the church fathers for women and the mother goddess archetype. In societies with less paranoid attitudes, the breast causes no such problems, whatever its size. Among the Trobriand Islanders, for instance, when anthropologist Bronislaw Malinowsky wrote his famous study, *The Sexual Life of Savages*, the women regularly went bare-breasted and the men showed no nervous or hostile overreaction. Evidently this was because the Trobrianders had no taboo on infant sexuality, no taboo on child sexuality, no recognition of a stage called "adolescence," no taboo on unmarried sexuality, and they modified their taboo on adultery by one of the easiest divorce systems ever recorded by ethnology. (A man who wanted *out* just moved out, and went to live with his brothers. A woman who wanted divorce put her husband's sandals outside the tent and he couldn't enter thereafter. If either party wanted to continue the marriage after such a breach, relatives would be sent to present gifts and arguments to persuade the other to relent.)

Obviously, the nipples on a passing female may have

stirred the fancies of a Trobriand male, but he was not chronically frustrated like many males in this society and did not go ape immediately. Malinowsky, in fact, could not find a single instance of rape or sex crimes of violence in the memory of his native informants, who, due to the tradition of verbal lore among preliterate peoples, could "remember" colorful or unusual events going back many generations. They could recall a few instances of homosexuality, which they thought were funny, and one or two suicides motivated by sexual jealousy, but no use of force between men and women. (In America, there is one rape every three minutes.) Possibly, given a good Christian education, these backward people would develop uptight and hostile reactions to visible breasts and, sooner or later, some native rapists and rippers would appear; this, after all, is the century of progress. Eventually, with the kind of luck we've had, they might even develop an autochthonous feminist movement to attribute such violence to "sexism" and urge the further repression of eros as a cure for the problem.

Some men, of course, will claim that the culturally acceptable rudeness to large-breasted women on our streets is not in any way related to the overt furies that possess rapists and rippers. They will even say that the women's liberationists, with their horror of every truck driver's wolf-whistle, sound like heroines of Victorian melodrama proclaiming the cosmic bathos of "Oh, sir, how dare you treat the flower of white womanhood this way!" One can sympathize with that cynical view, but the very same men (whisper the truth) will immediately recognize the hostility when such behavior is directed to a woman *they* happen to be escorting and will quickly whirl around with an angry shout of "Don't you jack-offs have anything better to do with your time?" or some more elegant *riposte*; or, if they don't show such protective anger the evening will be cursed with self-accusations of cowardice, will it not, O my brothers?

But in spite of such street-corner atavisms—which have

always plagued big cities: the 18th Century had young London hooligans known as "mohawks" whose pleasure was to throw pepper in the face of passers-by—the general tendency of the last decade is, at long last, to make a clean breast of it. In chic radical circles, and no less in shaggy hipster communes, the sight of a young mother nursing her infant in public is as commonplace as it was among the peasantry of old: the middle-class Victorian taboo here is almost dead. topless bars are still hounded by bluenoses, but still flourishing. The nipples which seemed a miracle in *Hawaii* can now be seen on almost any movie screen. More: even the old-fashioned "circus"—an orgy staged for the entertainment of spectators rather than for the enjoyment of the participants—can now be found far closer than Tijuana or Havana. It's a few blocks away, at a nightclub.

Not unexpectedly, as mammalphobia has declined, so have the other anal values and restrictions. The only minority which is not organized and fighting hard for its rights is the midgets, but there will probably be a Dwarf Liberation Front in existence by the time these words reach print. ("Power to the Little People!") No recent president has been able to come out in public without being met by signs, bluntly informing them that they are not universally beloved; a popular TV show (*All in the Family*) has presented a homosexual as a sympathetic, as distinguished from pitiful, character. You can't walk through the offices of any large corporation in the communication and entertainment fields without telltale odors revealing that somebody was smoking pot in his office. It is hard to resist the conclusion that Humpty Dumpty has fallen off the wall and not all the king's horses and all the pope's men can put him back together again.

And yet there was the explosion of Eleanor of Aquitaine and the troubadour poets once, and somehow, after the Albigensian Crusade, it was all put down and things returned more or less to normal. There was the Renaissance, when Venetian ladies sported bare breasts in public (rouge was applied to the nipples for further emphasis), and Michelangelo threw the pope off a scaffold for objecting to the nudity in his ceiling painting for the Sistine Chapel; when science broke loose from church control and explorers crossed space to new worlds and every painter did a voluptuous Venus in the nude (between chaste Virgin Marys for the town church); when humanists ironically watched the warfare between Catholic and Protestant and confidently expected that rationalism would triumph when the fanatics had all killed one another off. But once again the pendulum swung back much further than anyone had expected. Where do we actually stand now? He may answer who has the sociological calculus that will weigh the topless bars of San Francisco against the sporadic book-burnings that have recently occurred and the compulsory urine testing now in vogue.

A hundred years ago Charles Darwin wrote with great insight:

> In our maturer years, when an object of vision is presented to us which bears any similitude to the form of the female bosom . . . we feel a general glow of delight which seems to influence all our senses, and if the object be not too large, we experience an attraction to embrace it with our lips as we did in early infancy the bosom of our mothers.

This may be the process by which our ancestors were inspired to first sample such delicacies as apples, oranges, peaches, plums, grapefruit, maybe even watermelons. The pleasures of such fruit, of course, only serve to remind us unconsciously of what we really seek, but this is perhaps the association that led the Romans to provide grapes, wines and other oral delights at their sexual orgies. The oral mentality, and the peculiar tenderness that accompanies it, can be severely repressed, as 2000 years of Christianity have shown, but it cannot be exterminated.

The horrors of the first half of the 20th Century, coming

right after the general optimism of the late Victorian Age, have created an almost universal mood of skepticism and what Perls, Hefferline and Goodman, in *Gestalt Therapy*, call "chronic low-grade emergency"—escalating to genuine high-grade emergency every time the politicians start rattling their H-bombs threateningly. We are all more or less inclined to agree with Benjamin the Mule in Orwell's *Animal Farm*: "Things will go on as they always have, that is to say, badly." Almost every commentator on our sexual revolution, steeped in this atmosphere of gloom and doom, ends by predicting a swing of the pendulum back to the repressions of the past. And that was before AIDS.

It might be amusing, and even encouraging, to remind ourselves that the pendulum metaphor is only one way of scanning the future—other models are available. Robert A. Heinlein, the science-fiction writer, Alfred Korzybski, the semanticist, and R. Buckminster Fuller, the mathematician-designer, have all argued with great plausibility that the correct model with which to gauge technological trends is the *exponential curve*, the ever-rising skyrocket line that eventually goes off the top of the page and heads for infinity. There are reasons, all three of these writers have suggested, to think that social progress can also become steady and move in an ever-upward direction if certain blockages are removed. The first such roadblock to be cleared away, obviously, is the pessimistic assumption that this is impossible and that we must resign ourselves to a downward dip of the pendulum.

So: If we look into our crystal ball with an optimistic bias for once, we can discern the outlines of a future that might exist and which will be a lot more pleasant than the past. For one thing, after the big if (*if* we don't blow ourselves to hell), modern technology is fairly sure to abolish extreme poverty and make the present living standard of the average middle-class white American the bottom level standard of the world; many will live above that. Revolutions after that point will not be raggedy peasants shouting "We want bread," but well-dressed and well-educated people shouting,"We want more freedom to make our decisions"— and they will be shouting it at both socialist commissars and capitalist legislators. Such libertarian insurrections can only lead to more liberty, not (as has too often been the case in past revolutions) to less liberty.

The philosophy of hedonism, always subject to attack as "heartlessly selfish" in the past, will not have that drawback in such an economy of abundance. Repression of all sorts will appear more and more foolish. The simple statement of the French Revolutionaries of 1789—"every person has the right to do that which harms not others"—will be understood more and more as the basic axiom of social living-together, and all exceptions will have to be justified as very obvious and clear-cut emergency measures under decidedly special circumstances. Hopefully, most people will be very suspicious of such emergencies and will tend to support the accused individualist instead of the angry mob. Any arguments that a man or woman should not do any *harmless* thing that comes into their heads will be forced to justify itself on better grounds than the repressive forces of the past have ever promulgated. The "pursuit of happiness," stated as a goal in our Declaration of Independence, will be accepted as the normal attitude. In the age-old debate between Desire and Authority it is Authority that (at last) will be on the defensive.

Heinlein and Fuller, extrapolating from the growing tolerance of nudity on European beaches (which has now reached parts of California) and the advances in heating technology, have both predicted that nudity will be more commonplace than clothing in the near future. Presumably, the latter will be ceremonially continued in certain religious or political rituals, just as, according to many anthropologists, clothing was originally invented not for shelter from the elements but to indicate people's various functions in ritual relationships of religion, marriage, war, etc. (The old gimmick, often given in character-building or self-help books, of *seeing* a threatening person such as a boss or tax official standing in his underdrawers as he talks to you, is based on the fact that clothing is, indeed, one of the chief reinforcers of our social roles and games.) A nude society, almost certainly, will be more psychologically egalitarian than any we have known, whether it be economically socialist or capitalist or (as seems the trend) mixed.

Sex, obviously, will be considered one of the arts, rather then one of the problems, of life. The Oriental attitude toward eros, which might be described as, "This is good; let's see how much better we can make it," will bit by bit replace the puritanical, "This is bad; let's see how much worse we can make it." The attitude of the Tantric cults within Hinduism and Buddhism, which as we have seen, has already played an underground role in Western history, will be more readily acceptable and will not have to disguise itself as "alchemy" or "magick." (Perhaps it won't even have to disguise itself as psychotherapy.) This Tantric philosophy was well summarized in a memorable passage in Aleister Crowley's *Book of the Law*:

> Be not animal; refine thy raptures. If thou dine, dine by the eight and ninety rules of art; if thou love, exceed by delicacy; and if thou do aught joyous, let there by subtlety therein. . . . The word of sin is Restriction.

In short, the sexual Epicure will be no more brutish or hasty than the gourmet; and in an economy of abundance, with nothing in dwindling supply except repression, the trend will be for all to approach sex in an Epicurean manner. Dalliance, which is the most pleasant word for sex in the present English vocabulary, will become the rule rather than the rare exception. Almost certainly, the haste shown in Kinsey's 1940s averages was largely caused by a desire to get the act over before both parties had to face consciously that what they were doing was officially considered "dirty," just as Brutus in *Julius Caesar* wanted the assassination completed quickly so that he wouldn't have to contemplate the horror of the deed. When sex is not considered somewhat worse that murder, such fumbling furtiveness will vanish. Reports that Tantric Hindus can continue the act for seven hours or longer may be wickedly exaggerated, but in this happy future more than a small minority of Westerners will be inclined to find out the limits for themselves.

The breasts, of course, have been explored by the voluptuous for millennia and one would expect that their possibilities have been rather thoroughly plumbed. In true dalliance, however, as every pot smoker will assure you, there are new discoveries to be made every night. The hands, the mouth and the penis can be applied to the breasts at different times for an endless variety of charming results. For instance—

The hands. Cupping, gentle squeezing, rubbing, etc., with the entire palm and fingers is, or should be, known to everybody. But the fingers alone have many interesting possibilities. Any man who has ever had the delight of enjoying the sensations while his lady traces the circle around the head of his penis with *one finger*, again and again, around and around, knows that this pleasure becomes almost excruciating in only a few moments, and almost as intense as fellatio if one is able to continue it for a long period. The same single finger approach to a nipple can be equally transcendent for some ladies, especially if another finger or two or three are busy in the vulva at the same time. Like all sexual specialties, this is best if both parties consider it a treat in itself and not part of the build-up to the main event. Copulation is certainly one of nature's greatest inventions, but, as Norman O. Brown showed in *Life Against Death*, Western sexuality has been appallingly impoverished by the notion that everything else is only part of the progression to that grand climax. To shift the mood in a more languid and Oriental direction, practitioners of the more occult sexual arts often use a Hindu or Japanese musical accompaniment. This sort of music, in which every note is equally important and nothing is structured *à la* Beethoven to build toward a thundering conclusion, perfectly expresses the total immersion in each moment which is the essence of Oriental sensuality.

Similarly, the other portions of the breast—and, indeed, the whole body—can become increasingly sensitive to the meanderings of one single finger. A couple exploring this ocean of sensation with a Raga background provided by the stereo can easily drift off into an approximation of hypnogogic trance (the state just before sleep or, if you don't leap out of bed at the sound of an alarm, right after sleep) in which the usual visual orientation of our culture is slightly suspended and—even without drugs—one can begin to grasp what McLuhan means by "tactile involvement," what Freud meant by "oceanic experience," and what Norman O. Brown has dared to call "the resurrection of the body." Three dimensional space, which modern physics and modern neurology now know to be a creation of our visual cortex, easily expands into multidimensional sensory space such as the esthetically sensitive can enter by closing their eyes when listening to Bach or Vivaldi; but in the case of skillful sexual dalliance one enters this realm through all-over body feelings and not merely through the ear aided by imagination.

The mouth. Actual sucking on the nipples is, naturally, most appealing to the oral element in all of us, but it need not exhaust one's imagination. The varieties of kissing can be explored endlessly. There is the slow, languid kiss which after a few moments is more exciting to the kisser that the kissee. There is the chicken-peck technique—a series of very short kisses tracing a path, say from one nipple up to the neck, or lips, and back down to the other nipple. There are combinations and permutations of long slow kisses and short pecky ones—with love, lust and enough imagination, one can easily create patterns as intricate as a Bach fugue or a

Mondrian abstraction, and in what better area than this can an otherwise inartistic man express his esthetic sense? There are a variety of patterns to be experimented with—circles around the nipples, ellipses around the perimeter of the breasts themselves, straight lines and geodesic lines, and so on, endlessly. Variations in speed and tempo can prolong this far beyond any point the "Minute Man" of Kinsey's day could imagine.

Actual licking, however delightful for the male, is somewhat problematical. A wet area on the nipple or elsewhere on the breast becomes a distraction or annoyance for the woman quite quickly. Licking should be kept to a minimum or reserved entirely for points south, since any wet spot *outside* the nude body is a cold spot. If one can't resist licking, however, one should use the same principles of varying tempos and patterns as in kissing, and then ask the lady if she's feeling a chill and offer to dry her with a corner of the bedding. This last detail—asking about the other party's reactions—is an important general principle, incidentally, and most sexual resentments or maladjustments are caused by fear of asking such questions or the reverse fear of volunteering such information because it might appear as a complaint. A great poet once said, "Peace comes of communication." So does sexual gratification. *Silence is the chief tool of the resentful oral neurotic (just as severing diplomatic relations is always the first move toward war)*, and too much atmosphere of cathedral quietude in a love affair is a warning that both parties are communicating with their own fantasies and not with each other.

The penis. Most Americans still seem to be unaware that anything which can be done with a finger can also be done with the penis. In particular, penis-nipple conjunctions are a great deal more fun than finger-nipple manipulations. One can also trace patterns around the nipples, around the breasts, up to the neck, the lips, the earlobes, etc., all of which can be continued with mutual delight for quite a long time before moving on to other divertissements.

More amusing is intermammary intercourse. Here I can do no better than quote the instructions provided by Dr. Alex Comfort in his wonderfully explicit book, *The Joy of Sex*:

> Lay her half flat on pillows, kneel astride (big toe to her clitoris if she needs helping) and your foreskin fully retracted. Either you or she can hold the breasts together. Wrap them around the shaft rather than rub the glans with them. It should protrude clear, just below her chin. And orgasm from this position, if she gets one, is "round," like the full coital orgasm and she feels it inside. Breast orgasms from licking and handling are "in between" in feel. Rub the semen well into her breast when you have finished
>
> Skin is our chief extragenital sexual organ—grossly underrated by most men, who tend to concentrate on the penis and clitoris. . . .
>
> Intercourse between the breasts is equally good in other positions—head to tail or with her on top (especially if she has small breasts) or man sitting, woman kneeling; experiment accordingly.[35]

Even better, of course, is the combination of intermammary intercourse and fellatio. In this case, the penis does not "protrude . . . just below the chin" but reaches up into the mouth. This can easily be managed, without stretching into yogalike positions and getting strained muscles, if the couple are willing to experiment a bit. Best bet, in most cases, is for the lady to kneel (on a pillow) and the man to sit on the edge of the bed leaning forward slightly. If she has long hair, he can run his hands through it during this enchantment, with an added fillip for both of them.

In the free society we envision, such enjoyments will be no more concealed or surrounded with fear than baseball or ballet is. If a million radicals arrive in Washington to demonstrate against Social Security, the president will not put them down by announcing he was watching football, but by saying that he was enjoying the *Yokahoma Sex Specialty*

Show on satellite. Aldous Huxley's famous guess about the conversation of a sexually free utopia, in *Brave New World*, might also come true and the best way to describe a lady might be to say, as in that novel, "She's very pneumatic." And, of course, Huxley's amusing use of that adjective had a precedent which no doubt inspired him, for T.S. Eliot had already expressed such a tactile awareness (as McLuhan would call it) in his poem *Whispers of Immortality*, where he refers to the "promise of pneumatic bliss" in Grishkin's bust.

Such a tactile, pneumatic society, sensually and sensorily oriented, will obviously continue the current fads of rich fabrics, incenses, psychedelic art and the general paraphernalia of Consciousness III. If this is a picture of a largely oral population, they at least will be oral in the manner of Jesus and Shakespeare, *rather than in the spiteful and neurotic manner of those who harbor oral personalities in our largely antioral culture of recent times.* Those who still speak for the dying anal-patrist value system will denounce this forecast as dreadfully materialistic, but actually it transcends both spirituality and materialism as those therms have traditionally been understood in the West. Like the Orient, it will be profoundly existential, centered on those immediate experiences which are too deep, too oceanic, too real, to be classified as simply material or simply spiritual. Modern Hindus, still reeling from the impact of puritanical English conquerors, often try to sound more "spiritual" in a dualistic sense than any Christian prude, but their traditional sacred texts are quite explicitly existentialist and nondualist. The *Chandogya Upanishad* for instance says:

> Man issues forth from bodily identification to assume his real form upon attainment of the great liberation. Such a man lives like a king—eating, playing, and enjoying women, possessions, and family, without identification with the body.

This is exactly the attitude of the "eight and ninety rules of art" in Aleister Crowley's *Book of the Law*:

Be goodly therefore; dress ye in fine apparel; eat rich foods and drink sweet wines that foam! Also, take your fill and will of love as ye will, when where and with whom ye will!. . . But ecstacy be thine and joy of the earth. . . . For pure will, unassuaged of purpose, delivered from the lust of result, is every way perfect.

"The lust of result," the anal preoccupation with time and schedule, produced not only the mournful one-and-a-half minute copulations recorded by Kinsey but the titanic abuse of technology that created our staggering ecological problem. Such an attitude is not materialistic any more than the woman-hating and witch-burning churchmen were truly spiritualistic. When the problem of poverty is solved (and Buckminster Fuller has published detailed programs of how it could be solved within a decade if the politicians ceased blocking the natural tendency of worldwide technology), human society will cease to resemble the struggles of bull seals fighting for territory at mating time. Then, when we are able to look at each other without fear and calculation, the latent paranoia behind such anal compulsions will be seen for what it is. Probably, like people on their first acid trip, we will spend a long time laughing at what fools we have been.

As we live more and more in this oceanic-sensory Consciousness III and the truncated and partial awareness typical of traditional spirituality or materialism becomes more and more a memory of a deluded past, we will eventually face the question raised so jarringly by writers like Marcuse and Brown and Leary: is it possible for society to exist entirely without repression? History—the nightmare from which we are all trying to awake, in Joyce's memorable phrase—emphatically says no; but when we have finally awakened will another answer be possible? What are the dangers of appetite when the economy of scarcity and the culture of Puritanism have both died? In the workless society foreseen by Fuller and the cyberneticists, what will remain to distract men and women from the ever-expanding consciousness which, according to all yogis, eventually culminates in universal love?

This question, of course, has to be left open at present. Meanwhile, we can at least say that the mysterious link between sex and religion, which every sensitive person has noticed in one way or another, may contain a lot more than is evident in the familiar Freudian conclusion that religion is "only" sublimated sex. As Norwegian psychotherapist Ola Raknes writes in his *Wilhelm Reich and Orgonomy*, discussing an earlier book in which he had attempted to explain mysticism scientifically:

> The first thing I tried to show was that the so-called "mystical states of consciousness" can be rationally explained as irruptions into consciousness of repressed thoughts and emotions in such a way that they were not felt as originating in the person himself. . . . To a certain extent that may be correct, but the chief thing that breaks through is *the feeling of (energetic) streamings* in the body, the *elation* accompanying these streamings, the overwhelming feeling of *being moved by something outside one's conscious self,* and the feeling of *experiencing a new kind of life.* [Italics mine.]

Here, at the conclusion of this book, I am willing to say quite frankly that on one occasion, when I took the peyote cactus (source of mescaline) with a Sioux Indian friend, and on a second occasion, when I was given three lessons in kundalini yoga by a Hindu visitor to the United States, I have experienced what Dr. Raknes is talking about here. I have also had milder, but increasingly intense, experiences of it in the sexual embrace. Never have I felt any need to attribute it to being possessed by a god or goddess, a Buddha or a Bodhisattva, or even by dear old Crowley's mysterious "Holy Guardian Angel"; nor am I totally convinced that one must, like Reich, posit an entirely new and unknown energy source to account for it—the known bioelectric forces might be merely magnified in a synergetic way, as Fuller's mathematics seems to suggest. Nevertheless, it is quite definitely a streaming, a very unique elation accompanying the streaming (banishing all possibility of despair or depression for weeks afterward), an unmistakable sensation of being "*moved by something outside one's conscious self*" (to continue Dr. Raknes's description, and, above all, "*the feeling of experiencing a new kind of life*." Some such sensations are part of every satisfactory orgasm, of course, but to a much milder degree. Examples of what I am trying to convey: when Shakespeare wrote of orgasm as "the momentary trick" (in *Measure for Measure*) he had not yet experienced this kind of orgasm; when Hemingway wrote the much-mocked passage in *For Whom the Bell Tolls* about "feeling the earth move," he obviously *had* (and those who have mocked it, like the critics of Lawrence's sex scenes, obviously haven't).

"The feeling of experiencing a new kind of life" is the very essence of this experience. "Awakening," "Enlightenment" and "Illumination" are the terms most commonly used by mystics, and those who have reached the highest peaks were called "*digenes*" (twice-born) in the ancient Greek cults of Dionysus and "born again" in Christianity. A few weeks ago I attended a Fundamentalist service in San Francisco, ostensibly Christian, in which all the traditional methods of tribal shamanism were conspicuously present—dancing, singing, hand-clapping, rhythmic swaying, all in an ever-louder and ever-faster movement toward crescendo. This continued for three hours and then "miraculous" cures and cases of "possession by the Spirit" began to erupt all around the hall, each one triggering two or three others. And if I wasn't convinced that "the Lord Jesus" was present, as everybody was shouting to everybody else, I don't think such footless phrases as "auto-suggestion" or "crowd psychology" quite explain it either. The diehard rationalist who says this is all "only mental" might as well try to convince me that orgasm itself is "only mental." One might as well tell the adolescent boy and girl who are experiencing coitus for the first time that what is happening is "all in your head." They know that what is happening is not at all comparable to the "only mental" act of fantasizing about sex, just as eating a meal is not comparable to reading the menu.

This book has been written with laughter and love, and if I sometimes seem critical of those people and institutions who are guided more by gloom and bitterness—the misogynists who so often have turned the gentle religion of Jesus into a spectacularly bloody hate-trip, the misanthropists who have reduced the perfectly legitimate cause of women's liberation to the shrill crackles of witches laying a very bad whammy on the world—it is only because I think this ecstasy (from the Greek *ec-stasis*, out of oneself) is our human birthright and should not be taken from us. Abbie Hoffman's simple-minded mantra, "You can't do good unless you feel good," does not seem less true to me as I grow older, but more true. I don't mind sounding corny at times, and I say quite frankly that what the world needs most is a little more tenderness. It is not likely to get that from people who are perpetually programming themselves (and others) with fear, hostility, resentment and bitterness.

Sex is not the "central sacrament of life" as a few ultrahip modern poets have said. It is a late arrival in the story of evolution, and even though it perpetuates all the higher species, it is obviously of only peripheral emotional importance to them—except at mating season when they can sometimes act as foolish as you or I and when even the gentle deer will fight among themselves. The process that made us human, however, did move sex into a new importance, spreading it outward from the genitals to many other areas of the body, as we have seen, and paralleling this growth-in-space with a growth-in-time that eventually included the whole solar year. If it is not central to all life, it emphatically is central to humanity, and if evolution is continuing, it will become even more important in ways that we can scarcely begin to imagine.

Psychic healers who use sexual energy consciously, such as Rasputin or Aleister Crowley, have been rare in our civilization, although he Chinese Taoists never made any secret of the libidinal source of their power. I have no doubt that the kundalini force which my Hindu teacher partially awakened in me was the same force stirred up in the mass audience of the Christian faith healer whose vibes I described a few pages back, Hindus have never denied that the kundalini is a sexual force, even though some of them, still reeling from the impact of Victorian English administrators on their society, prefer to speak in public only about the nonsexual and indirect ways of rousing the "serpent" in the chakras of the autonomic nervous system. The Shaivite and Tantric sects of Hinduism, meanwhile, have always continued to use the direct sexual methods, however much this may horrify Occidental visitors to their land.

There is cosmic humor, a jest for the gods, in the fact that these prudish visitors will often, despite their horror, snap a roll of photographs of the erotic carvings in the Black Temple and bring them home to show all their friends. Denying that this erotic force is spiritual, speaking of it (in direct contradiction of the evolutionary facts) as an "animalistic" part of mankind, yet they are moved by it. There is cosmic tragedy, to make the angels weep, in the fact that they experience this stirring deep within only as—in D.H. Lawrence's fine phrase—"the dirty little secret."

As long as the breasts remain part of the "dirty little secret," ours will be a fundamentally irrational society. Indeed, as long as any part or function of humanity remains hidden in obscenity, society will be partly mad. This is sad, of course, but not nearly as exceptional as is usually thought by those who, raised with the illusion that this is a rational and scientific civilization, suddenly discover how basically superstitious and absurd it really is. Actually, all human societies of which we have any record are slightly lunatic. If the locals do not worship snakes or bulls, they worship invisible demons and gods; if they are not terrified of nude breasts, they are worried that Friday is an unlucky day or that witches have put a curse on their cornfields. Men and women are imaginative beings, and they learned how to form theories very early in their evolution; few of them have yet learned how to criticize or validate their theories. Most religions make such criticisms a crime.

In contrast to our deliberately optimistic sketch of the future, the latest Supreme Court rulings on "obscenity" are a backward swing of the pendulum, just as cynics have long been predicting. Once again we are told that parts of our bodies must remain *dirty little secrets* and that the state will use its powers of coercion to enforce this code upon us. To a rationalist, it is as if the highest court had ruled that we must all believe, or pretend to believe, in the doctrine of the Trinity. Some people can believe in a three-in-one divinity, and some can believe that the human body is foul; others can no more believe these propositions than they can accept the tenets of the snake-handling cult in Georgia which we mentioned earlier. It doesn't matter what rationalists believe; they must not get caught exercising their disbelief. The only consolation is that things would be even more absurd if it were the snake handlers and not the sexophobes who were in power in Washington. There is, in fact, no reason why the notions of the snake handlers could not be enforced on the rest of us if they did get their crowd into high office, for as Mr. Justice Burger said in a recent decision (Paris Adult Theatre):

> But it is argued there is no scientific data which conclusively demonstrates that exposure to obscene materials adversely effects men and women or their society. It is urged on behalf of the petitioners that absent such a demonstration any kind of state regulation is "impermissible." It is not for us to resolve empirical uncertainties underlying state legislation save in the exceptional case where that legislation plainly impinges upon

rights protected in the Constitution itself . . . although there is no conclusive proof of a connection between anti-social behavior and obscene materials, the legislature of Georgia could quite reasonably determine that such a connection does or might exist. In deciding Roth, this Court implicitly accepted that a legislature could legitimately act on such a conclusion to protect "the social interest in order and morality" . . . . From the beginning of civilized societies, legislatures and judges have acted on various unproven assumptions.

In short, there is no need to prove that an act is harmful to prohibit it. If the legislators choose to prohibit it, the citizenry must acquiesce—or go to jail.

As Wayland Young had pointed out:

But it is difficult or even impossible to argue that the accepted limits of obscenity should themselves be redrawn without actually infringing them in the process, and having to defend one's argument against a charge of obscenity. In this case, one would have to prove affirmatively that a discussion of the public interest was in the public interest, which is a startling thing to have to prove in a democracy.

The effect is naturally that the present conception of the public interest becomes sacrosanct. If I merely say, speaking generally, "We call too may things obscene, we are too restrictive in our definitions," nobody will pay any attention, and our conception of the public good will remain unchanged. If, on the other hand, I give examples, saying: "Consider these," and give my reasons for thinking they ought not to be held obscene, my book may be suppressed for obscenity before anybody has had time to consider it, and our conception of the public good will still remain unchanged. Our society has painted itself into a corner . . . the law of obscenity has the indirect effect of perpetuating itself. *You cannot argue with it without breaking it.*[36] [Italics in original.]

This is all very absurd, because within the criteria used in modern science and modern semantics *the concept of "obscenity" must be regarded as a delusion.* That is, it is a nonoperational concept, one which cannot be utilized in making measurements of the physical world—there is no "obscenometer" which can point at a book or a painting or a song or a film and take a reading showing how many ergs or ounces of "obscenity" it has in it. There is no "obscenity" in any of these things, in fact; the "obscenity" is in the mind of the person passing judgments. It is, in Freudian terms, a projection, in which the mind imagines that its own contents are outside itself in the external universe; or, in semantic terms, a "confusion of the levels of abstraction," in which the mind's own machinery is identified with the non-mental things it is attempting to understand. The man or woman who believes there is something called "obscenity" out there in the external world is thus in precisely the same state of delusion as those who imagine that gods or demons or strange voices out there are communicating with them. As psychologist Theodore Schroeder insisted, the belief in external "obscenity" is the modern form of the witchcraft delusion.

This realization that our learned legislators and judges are not much different from madmen in some respects should not surprise us too much. We have seen, throughout this book, that attitudes toward the covering and uncovering, emphasis or de-emphasis, adoration or fear, of the breast are all based on various superstitious ideas. In ancient Egypt, evidently, woman and the moon were the original religious objects because their mutual 28-day periods were the earliest markers of time. When the cycles of solar time were discovered, the male sun god, Osiris, and the male phallus, became sacred, and woman and the moon were pushed into second place. Eventually, under Christianity, the female-lunar rites became identified with witchcraft and black magic, and their appearance provoked the horror and hatred of the great witch-hunts. It is within this context that the Christian feeling that the breast is "obscene" must be understood. (Similarly, the use of drugs in the lunar-female religions explains the Christian antipathy to drugs.)

"A change in language can transform our appreciation of the cosmos," said the semanticist and metalinguist Benjamin Lee Whorf. On pages 57-59, I illustrated how the concept of anality, dirt, smut, etc., is attached to the genitals or the breasts by chains of semantic association, just as, in earlier religions, concepts of holiness, divinity, beauty, etc., were semantically linked with these organs. It is difficult for human beings to see that these associations are inside their own heads; it is difficult not to see the associations *outside attached to the organs themselves.* It is especially difficult to understand that somebody else, looking at the same breasts or genitals, might see entirely different associations; the usual reaction is to think that somebody else is mad or perverse. This is the tragedy of humanity and the cause of most of our wars and persecutions.

Let us listen a moment to the wise words of T. Clifton Longworth:

> Pagan philosophy, moreover, taught that there is nothing under the sun more sacred than physical love, and nothing more beautiful than the human body. The great festivals of the love-goddesses were the wonders of the ancient world. At Athens, Corinth, Paphos, Ballbek and a hundred other sacred shrines great multitudes flocked to the festivals of the goddess, for the Worship of Love. To the pilgrims of that era the rites of Aphrodite were as simple, as natural, as joyous, and as remote from the idea of sin as the mating of the birds. . . .
>
> It is an amusing fact that Catholics regard the lovely white blossom of the lily as a symbol of purity, yet it is the sex organ of the plant. How then can sex be ugly and disgusting? It is to it we owe the song of the nightingale, the painted wings of the butterfly, the gorgeous plumage of the bird of paradise and the blush and perfume of the rose. It is love, too, which has inspired the greatest works of poets, painters, artists, and musicians; while among myriads of humbler folk it has gilded drab homes with beauty and has brought light and joy into the darkest lives.[37]

It does appear to a rationalist that by making this view-point illegal (or actions based on this viewpoint illegal), and by writing a Christian code into our laws, the courts and legislators have violated the First Amendment provision against "the establishment of religion." The bluenoses, of course, cannot make us believe that sex is really ugly and dirty (but even the Holy Inquisition could not literally make the heretics believe in orthodoxy); yet they have the power to force us to act as if we shared their antisexual hangups. As Wayland Young says, this is startling in a democracy; and yet it has happened, again and again, since the dawn of the Republic. Perhaps the iron wall between church and state should have been reinforced steel.

Nevertheless, the rosy future we have portrayed is not impossible, only improbable. By and large, the cliché about a "generation gap" is true: The exponents of the old-time morality are generally aged people, and Consciousness III is mostly the property of the young. However many years the Reagan Court may survive Reagan, we still have the reassurance once offered by the English underground paper, *It*: "Every minute, more and more of them die off; every minute, more and more of us are born." A society based on love and freedom is, as it has always been, possible. Some-day, maybe not next August but maybe the August after, the influence of the young may become stronger than the influence of the old and we may be able to begin building a society in which the dirt and smut thrown on the breasts and the rest of the human body will finally be washed off. Let us look forward to that golden dawn. We have lived too long in the dark.

[34] *Ms.*, August 1972.

[35] Alex Comfort, *The Joy of Sex* (New York: Crown Publishers, 1972).

[36] Young. *op. cit.*

[37] T. Clifford Longworth, *The Gods of Love; Creative Process in Early Religion* (Westport, Conn.: Associated Booksellers, 1960).

Robert Anton Wilson's Newsletter...
Trajectories

Trajectories is your kind of reading if you're interested in creating the future instead of worrying about it...

Trajectories is for you if you are deeply interested in...Our future in space....Nanotechnology and artificial intelligence....Parapsychology....Longevity....the new brain machines...the Aquarian Conspiracy

Trajectories is ~~tomorrow's news today~~

Edited by Robert Anton Wilson (with Arlen Riley Wilson and D. Scott Apel),**Trajectories** will bring you the latest news from the cutting edge of science & technology... Wilson's own unique humor...and much, much more...interviews with **Timothy Leary, Barbara Marx Hubbard, Linus Pauling** and many other innovators and pioneers...Feminist Futurism by Arlen Riley Wilson...a chat with the readers by RAW himself in every issue

For the first year, **Trajectories** will appear quarterly, and. we hope to increase it to monthly publication thereafter. If you subscribe for two years now, you will receive all issues for the first 24 months.

Subscription: $20 for 1 year/ $35 for 2 years/$50 for 3 years
Make checks payable to: **Permanent Press**

Permanent Press
PO Box 700305
San Jose, CA 95170

YES, I want to subscribe to <u>Trajectories.</u>
Enclosed is my check for ____ for __ years.

Name:_____
Address: _____
City & State: _____Zip Code_____

What critics say about Robert Anton Wilson

A super-genius . . . He has written everything I was afraid to write.

Dr. John Lilly

Stupid

Andrea Antonoff

the man's either a genius or Jesus

SOUNDS (London)

a 21st Century Rennaisance Man . . . funny, wise and optimistic . . . the Lenny Bruce of philosophers.

DENVER POST

the world's greatest writer-philosopher

Irish Times (Dublin)

hilarious . . . multi-dimensional . . . a laugh a paragraph

Los Angeles Times

ranting and raving . . . negativism . . .

Neal Wilgus

one of the most important writers working in English today . . . courageous, compassionate, optimistic and original.

Elwyn Chamberling, author of Gates of Fire

should win the Nobel Prize for INTELLIGENCE
QUICKSILVER MESSENGER (Brighton)

Wilson managed to reverse every mental polarity in me, as if I had been dragged through infinity. I was astounded and delighted.

Philip K. Kick, author of Blade Runner

one of the leading thinkers of the modern age
Barbara Marx Hubbard
Committee for the Future

A male feminist . . . a simpering, pussy-whipped wimp
Lou Rollins

sexist

Arlene Meyers

The most important philosopher of this century . . . scholarly, witty, hip and hopeful

Timothy Leary

What great physicist hides behind the mask of "Robert Anton Wilson?"

New Scientist

Does for quantum mechanics what Durrell's *Alexandria Quarteet* did for Relativity, but Wilson is funnier
John Gribbin, physicist

Obscene, blasphemous, subversive and very, very interesting
Alan Watts

erudite, witty and genuinely scary
Publishers Weekly

deliberately annoying
Jay Kinney

Misguided malicious fanaticism
Robert Sheafer,
Committee for Scientific Investigation
of Claims of the Paranormal

The man's glittering intelligence won't let you rest. With each new book, I look forward to his wisdom, laced with his special brand of crazy humor
Alan Harrington, author of The Immortalist